BURIED BENEATH THE BOARDING HOUSE

A SHOCKING TRUE STORY OF DECEPTION, EXPLOITATION AND MURDER

RYAN GREEN

Disclaimer

This book is about real people committing real crimes. The story has been constructed by facts but some of the scenes, dialogue and characters have been fictionalised.

Polite Note to the Reader

This book is written in British English except where fidelity to other languages or accents are appropriate. Some words and phrases may differ from US English.

For Helen, Harvey, Frankie and Dougie

CONTENTS

Mama Knows Best

The first time that Peggy came to the house on F Street, she had no idea what to expect. Usually, the lodging houses in Sacramento that were willing to take in the homeless and the addicted were one bad day away from demolition — some slum lord's last attempts to squeeze a few more dollars out of a dying neighbourhood before the whole thing got bulldozed for a strip-mall.

F Street was a quiet stretch of suburbia. There were kids playing in the streets, riding their bikes up and down the sidewalk and selling nothing more intoxicating than lemonade on the street corners. When she pulled up outside, with no companion but a heap of overflowing manila folders in the passenger seat, she had to stop and double-check that she was in the right place.

The house at 1426 F Street was a two-story Victorian building standing tall and proud behind a well-tended garden. The paintwork on the outside of the house was just as immaculate as the lawn; pristine enough that it gave Peggy a twinge of guilt about the state of her own fairly well-maintained house.

Something about this picture didn't add up — there was no desperation in the air, no sign that this was the last stop before the graveyard. A lodging house like this could demand far more than the pitiful stipend that the state paid to house its down and outs. It could be a private care home, a hotel or even something more. It was only when she came closer that it started to add up.

There was a big man in the garden, heavily tattooed and more than a little intimidating as he moved among the flower beds with his muscles rippling. There was only one place that a man got top-heavy like that — prison. It was incongruous, watching him carefully planting delicate flowers with hands so big and scarred. He gave a deferring nod to Peggy as she passed but was careful not to stare at her legs, even as they went right by his face. An ex-con who intended to stay free; someone else who was down on their luck, being offered a second chance at life by whoever operated this boarding house.

The door had opened before Peggy could knock, and she'd flinched back from the smell of liquor rolling off the man who loomed out at her. He was shorter than her, wearing clean but badly-worn clothes, and he had the yellow tint of a failing liver in the whites of his eyes. Both of them froze in surprise, then he bellowed over his shoulder, 'Mrs D. Somebody to see you!'

Peggy was ushered in and took in the sights and sounds with something approaching awe. The house was full of music. A record player spun in the corner of the living room, and Spanish singing drifted out through the open front door. There was a party atmosphere in the main room, and while none of the residents seemed to be drinking, they were all enjoying each other's company. There was a card game going on the coffee table, and two older women sat by the bay windows chattering away. A man was sitting alone on the floral sofa, staring into space; even his foot was tapping along to the tune. Every one of the people in the house showed some hint at their true nature. From the spasmodic twitching of one old woman to the quiet muttering of the man in the corner, each of them hinted at some deep-rooted problem that would have them turned out of any 'decent establishment' after their first outburst. Yet, here, they seemed to be flourishing. The interior of the house was in good repair, even if the style was a little outdated, and there was the unmistakable smell of home-cooked Mexican food drifting through from the kitchen. The guests seemed more like a loosely assembled family than a group of addicts, mental patients and down and outs crammed into a building together. This place felt like a home. All of that had been more than a year ago, but when Dorothea opened the door to her with a big toothless smile, Peggy felt like it could've been yesterday.

'Miss Peggy! Come in, come in. Let me get you a coffee. It's been too long. You're here to see Bert?'

Coming into the presence of Dorothea Puente was like being enveloped in a grandmotherly hug. Peggy could easily understand why the woman found it so easy to keep tensions between all of her guests under control when her presence seemed to be so naturally calming. She had such faith in everyone she met, and it felt criminal to let her down. Even correcting her on something so minor felt strange. 'Uh, no, not today. I'm meant to be visiting a Mister Alvaro Montoya.'

'Yes, Alvaro is Bert. I don't know why. Come on through to my kitchen. He is helping me in there today.'

On a stool by the table, Bert sat shelling peas and muttering to himself in Spanish. He should have struck an imposing figure, but just like Dorothea, he radiated peace. Peggy knew that the muttering was a symptom of his schizophrenia — the voices that only he could hear; ones that he felt compelled to answer out of some misguided politeness. But, that wasn't the end of Bert's troubles. He was mentally disabled — a grown man on the outside but little more than a child behind his deep-set eyes. His schizophrenia had made care workers nervous. He was too unpredictable in their eyes to be safely homed with other developmentally stunted adults. Meanwhile, his disability had made him incapable of navigating the all-too-complex and dangerous world of mental health wards and medication balancing. Caught between these two pillars of social care, he had fallen through the cracks and ended up living rough, until a volunteer had picked him up and slotted him back into the system.

It was the first time that Peggy had actually met the man in person; everything else had filtered through to her in reports and coffee room conversations. He seemed every bit the gentle giant that had been promised to her, but it was all too possible that he was merely subdued because of the presence of an authority figure.

'Alvaro?'

He didn't look up from his bowl, still furiously arguing under his breath in a steady stream of Puerto Rican accented Spanish, too fast for anyone to understand him. Peggy tried again. 'Bert?'

His head jerked up suddenly, and it was all that she could do to stand her ground as his eyes slowly focused on her. A moment later, his face cracked into a beatific smile, and she let out the breath she didn't know she was holding. 'Hi there.' Peggy settled onto a stool beside Bert, taking care to move slowly and predictably. 'How are you doing, Bert?'

Even as they spoke, his hands were still moving, still shelling peas with mechanical efficiency. 'Helping Mama in the kitchen, today.'

'Such a sweet boy.' Dorothea's gummy grin spoiled her otherwise handsome face. 'So helpful around the house. I don't know what I would do if he ever left us.'

The rest of Peggy's questions were routine, but the answers that Bert gave her were still surprising. He showed a real understanding of his limitations, something that he had never really grasped before arriving in Dorothea's tender care. She took care of him in more ways than just filling his time and his stomach. His applications for social security had been rewritten to ensure he got all of the support that he was entitled to. Dorothea handled all of his money for him, providing him with spending money but keeping him from using it for anything too frivolous or destructive. Alcohol was officially banned for the residents of F Street, and without the liquor that Peggy assumed he'd been regularly consuming on the street, all of the symptoms of his schizophrenia seemed to be becoming more manageable. He was so calm and collected that Peggy wondered if they might not start him off on medication again to bring the whispering voices in his head completely under control.

By the time that their visit was done, Peggy couldn't keep her enthusiasm from showing. She wanted to hug Dorothea for what she'd done — something that a whole creaking net of social workers and carers had completely failed to do for years, if not decades.

With her interview complete, they retired to the living room, where the same record player was still spinning. She let at least a little of her excitement gush out. 'I can't believe what a difference you've made to that man's life. It goes above and beyond the charitable work you've been doing so far... you're not just housing him; you're teaching him how to live in the world. He isn't calling you 'Mama' out of delusion, or any belief that you're his birth parent — you've adopted that man!'

Dorothea feigned embarrassment. 'Oh, he's no trouble at all. I take care of all my friends in the house. He just needs a little more attention than some of the others.'

Peggy glanced around the empty room with a hint of a frown. 'Where are all your other residents, today? Every other time that I've visited, they've been in these communal areas.'

'It is very sad, but so many of them have moved on.' Dorothea let out a sigh. 'Some leave without a word, go back to the streets. Some move to a new town, new jobs, new dreams. I am happy for them, they're moving forwards with their lives, but I miss them.'

'It's a testament to the amazing work that you're doing here that so many of them are able to find their footing and start to rebuild their lives. You should be very proud.' Peggy leaned in and gave Dorothea's calloused hand a not terribly professional squeeze.

'Oh, no. It's no trouble at all. I just wish I could do more to help all of the people in this town who are in trouble. Perhaps...' She trailed off.

'Yes?'

Dorothea's eyes looked huge behind her thick glasses. 'If it's not too much trouble, perhaps you can send more people who need my help to stay? I have so many empty beds in this house, and there are so many people on the streets with nowhere to sleep at all.'

Peggy felt like her heart was swelling up. This woman wanted nothing more than to fill her home with the homeless, mentally ill and addicted. The ones that the rest of the world had left for dead. 'Oh, I promise you, after I report back on how well Alvaro is settling in here, you should have more applications than you can handle. I'll be personally recommending this place to everyone else in my department.'

Dorothea smiled again, looking every one of her 70 years as the wrinkles around her eyes threatened to consume her whole face. 'Thank you. You are so kind.'

There were some more pleasantries and some more pieces of paperwork to be signed off. But, before Peggy knew it, she was back on her feet and heading out the door, ready to dive back into the dark and dismal world that was her calling to help people navigate. The garden had changed yet again since the last time she was here. The ex-convicts that Dorothea so kindly employed had been set to work rearranging everything and planting a new tree near to the mailbox. There were mounds of fresh, turned earth everywhere that Peggy looked. She'd liked the garden just fine the way it was before, and she suspected that Dorothea only kept making changes so that she could keep paying money out to her gardeners, month after month. The woman was so generous; it was hard to believe.

With a genuine smile on her face for the first time in days, Peggy headed back to the car. She would find plenty of bodies to fill the spaces that Dorothea had made. She would make sure that the old woman's kindness was spread around to everyone who could receive it.

Born Alone

Redlands, California, was a town well on its way to being a city in 1929. The dustbowl days of the Great Depression had driven half the population of the central states in a great exodus across the California border, to the last place where the land was still green. Even little farming communities had gone, from crossroads general stores amidst the fields to burgeoning townships. The Native American and Mexican populations of Redlands had always been substantial compared to the number of late-arrival, white settlers, but now they were being drowned out by the itinerant workers who'd never moved on.

Navel oranges were the crop of choice, with sprawling orchards surrounding the town in every direction, covering 15,000 acres. The local workers, forced from their agricultural roles by the influx of new farmers, found themselves in the fruit packing warehouse, working long, sweltering hours for a fraction of what they used to be able to command for their skilled labour.

It was there that you might've expected to find Trudy Mae and Jesse James Gray, cramming oranges into crates and loading them on to trains, but that young couple had been told to never darken the factory's door again, after showing up drunk one time too many. They were both migrants to Redlands, carried along with the tide of jobseekers, despite sharing none of their experience with agriculture. They looked around at the dull and weary people around them and assumed that anyone could do the work. As it turned out, they couldn't. After being turned away from the fruit packing plant, Trudy couldn't find anyone to employ her, so the couple were left exclusively reliant on the pathetic amount that Jesse made picking cotton for a sharecropper, out a distance into San Bernardino County. Many days, he'd be too drunk to show up to work, so he wouldn't get paid. On the days that he did show up and get paid, he often drank his earnings before he even made it home.

Into this volatile household, on 9th January 1929, Dorothea Helen Gray was born. The sixth of seven children, she was predestined to be the last in line for everything. Despite being well-aware of her impending baby, Trudy hadn't slowed her drinking throughout the nine months of pregnancy, and it was to this that Dorothea's short stature could be ascribed. Even when she was breastfeeding Dorothea, the flow of liquor didn't stop, resulting in the baby spending most of her time in a silent stupor, wallowing in her own filth for hours at a time. For all that her mother's milk was tainted, at least it was consistent. When the time came for the child to move on to solid foods, there was rarely any to be had. Her older siblings taught her how to scavenge for scraps from a very young age, using the hungry toddler as a prop in their attempts to part neighbours from their food. When stories of their begging made their way back to Trudy, she was furious at her children 'shaming' her by behaving in that manner, and she was swift to apply corporal punishment to mend their ways.

The older children were accustomed to their mother's moods and knew that if they got out of reach and waited for her to work her way a little further down the day's bottle, then her fury would soon abate. They were quick on their feet and ready to dart out of the house at a moment's notice. Dorothea, barely able to walk at that age, was not so capable. She received all of the beatings that were intended for her siblings.

The vast majority of Trudy's anger was quite rightly directed at her husband, but he was never around to receive it, so that too was passed down to Dorothea. There was no real sadism in her treatment of the children, so much as there was a profound disinterest. Children were an unwanted chore in a life filled with unwanted chores, and while Trudy could muddle through when she had to, her preference was to pretend that the kids didn't exist at all. That way, she could focus on her far more important tasks, like the acquisition and consumption of as much alcohol as possible.

Jesse James Gray was a rare sight for his children, a sleeping body or a glowering tempest passing through the house on his way to work or a bar. The few interactions that he had with them were interspersed with bursts of violence. Trudy may not have cared about the children, but it was from a position of neutrality. Jesse seemed to actively despise the girls, and if they came into reach, he'd slap them just for the sake of doing them harm. He didn't want them around when he was at home, trying to take what little pleasure he could find in his wife, so the children were often banished en masse to the streets at night when he did find his way back home. These evening excursions were rare, but they provided the kids with an extra opportunity to scavenge for food, so they tried not to waste them.

The streets of Redlands were different in the dark. The white stonework of the municipal buildings took on a spectral quality by the moonlight, and the good-natured people that the children were likely to encounter through the day were all asleep in their beds.

Night was the time of the drunkard and the petty criminal. The dark shapes that they saw roaming the streets could have carried kindness or cruelty within them, of which the Gray kids had no hope of knowing until it was almost too late. They knew from their mother that a drunk could be capable of almost unimaginable acts of benevolence one moment and viciousness the next. Each time they tried for a handout, they knew the risk that they were running, and each time that things went wrong, it was Dorothea who was too slow on her feet to escape. The backhanded slaps intended to drive off the children would knock her into the gutter. The grasping hands that merely brushed her sister's skirts would lock onto her thighs. She was sexually assaulted on more than one occasion, but neither she nor her siblings would talk about it.

They were all uncomfortably familiar with the mechanics of sex — growing up in a single-roomed house with two horny alcoholics tends to be quite educational in that regard. But, they had also been indoctrinated thoroughly by their visits to church each week that sex was a wicked sin, and being party to it made her evil. Underlying that instilled guilt was the unavoidable truth that nobody really cared about them. They had been taught time and again that asking for help was tantamount to asking for trouble, so even when Dorothea suffered the most grotesque indignities, she did so in silence. As unlikely as it seems, things soon took a turn for the worse for Dorothea's family. After passing out drunk in the cotton fields one night, Jesse awoke the next morning soaked to the bone with a hacking cough. As the months stretched on, the cough got worse and worse until eventually his sleeve was perpetually stained with the blood that he wiped from his lips. It seemed like pneumonia, so the doctor prescribed him strict bed rest, cutting off the family's only source of income. Despite squandering the pittance of savings that they had left on medication, his condition did not improve. It was only in the final days of his confinement, when the priest and doctor were called around again, that the true diagnosis came to light: tuberculosis, which was lethal and contagious. The whole family had been exposed to the pathogen, and that made them a risk to the whole community.

The church was quick to furnish the family with food and alms for the duration of their months of quarantine — Dorothea's first lesson in the benefits of eliciting sympathy. But, as time rolled by without so much as a splutter from any one of the women, the flow of charity slowed to a trickle.

Jesse James Gray expired in the early months of 1937 with little fanfare. Dorothea was only eight years old when he was buried in the potter's field reserved for those too poor to afford a real funeral, but already any sense of sentimentality about the loss of her distant father was overwhelmed by the practicalities of her situation. With Jesse gone, so too had gone the family's only source of income, and while the people of Redlands were kind and sympathetic to the young widow, they weren't stupid enough to employ her.

Trudy soon took up with several different 'boyfriends' about town, each of whom provided her with a pittance in exchange for her company. The children spent more and more nights alone in the family home, fending for themselves and being considerably better off for their mother's absence. Often, those overnight stays would stretch out into weeks when they didn't see her, which were the nights when Trudy went straight from her appointments with men to the bar, trying to wash away the memories and tastes of what she had just done with rye whiskey.

Despite the absence of their mother, the kids muddled on, with the eldest learning the fundamentals of cooking and the youngest using their innocent appearance to beg with more efficiency. They had evening meals with many of the Mexican families in the neighbourhood, but always, Dorothea tried to pay her way by cleaning dishes and helping out in the kitchen. It was clear to everyone that Trudy was on a crash course with disaster, and before long, this prediction was proven more accurate than many would find palatable. A year after the death of her husband, while riding pillion on the back of a motorcycle with one of her 'clients', she was involved in a traffic accident. A car clipped the back wheel of the bike, sending it flying off the road and down a rocky slope. Even after it was retrieved, the body couldn't be made to look human again after such violent and repeated impacts.

When the police tracked the kids down and informed them of their mother's death, none of them seemed to be terribly surprised. If anything, they seemed relieved that they would no longer have to deal with her visits interrupting the tentative peaceful existence that they'd made for themselves.

Sadly, the children had no such luck. The apparatus of the state care system swung into lumbering effect, taking all seven of them into custody before scattering them to various orphanages that had spare beds. For the first time, Dorothea was completely alone, with none of her siblings for support and guidance. It didn't go well — the orphanages were grotesquely understaffed and underfunded, with a quality of food comparable to when Dorothea had been forced to dig through neighbour's bins for leftovers.

By the time that she turned ten, the following year, Dorothea's future started to look less bleak. One of her mother's sisters had finally been informed of Trudy's death, and she was set on adopting all of her nieces and nephews to get them out of care. It took several months to track each of the kids down, and considerably longer for all of the paperwork to be processed, but eventually, Dorothea was reunited with the only family members that had ever mattered to her.

In Fresno, California, Dorothea had the opportunity to start over, to set aside all of the horrors that she had suffered in her first decade of life and make new memories. Her older sisters, always the source of wisdom in her life, had begun doing exactly that, talking about their parent's death in a 'traffic accident' in vague terms and glossing over all of the horrific details of their life back in Redlands. They wanted to be normal girls, living normal lives, not victims of terrible circumstance. That was not enough for Dorothea, who'd suffered worse than any of them. Even the vague deceptions of her sisters were too close to the painful reality to endure. To feel truly safe in her new life, she had to create more distance from the past, so she set about cobbling together a whole new history for herself out of the only good memories she had —

those nights spent in the homes of Mexican families that seemed to care about her, and the loving embrace of her siblings.

When asked about her past, she fused and inflated those elements into a new life. She'd grown up in Mexico, in a family of 18 brothers and sisters, happy and loved, before coming to the States to start a new life. She would repeat that lie so many times through her life that it completely replaced the truth in her recollections. For a traumatised child, memory was a malleable thing, and that ceaseless repetition soon grew additional details about her home, her beloved sisters; her life. She learned Spanish to support her lie. She tried to blend into the Mexican community in Fresno, desperate to return to those happy memories of a place and time that never existed.

Love for Sale

The next few years of Dorothea's life were the most stable she'd ever had, and would ever experience. There was something resembling a support network for her in Fresno, between her new friends and her relatives. She flourished in that stability, attending school regularly for the first time, dressing herself in clean clothes and learning through a thousand little lessons that her childish cuteness was transforming into teenage beauty.

She could have built a new life for herself there on the breadline with her cousins and family if the heavy hand of the state had not intervened once more. There were far too many children in the house for the number of bedrooms, and while this was the greatest comfort that Dorothea had ever experienced, it was considered to be a danger to her and her siblings. They were removed from the family home and dispersed once more, not to orphanages but to foster homes across the state. Dorothea bounced from family homes to those of strangers, from Fresno to Los Angeles and on to

Napa, being uprooted over and over as the foster families that housed her discovered she was wilful and coarse when pushed. Dorothea bucked against any rules that were laid down for her, however reasonable. She couldn't understand the purpose of a curfew or why she needed to come straight home from school. She was used to coming and going as she pleased, and the restrictions being laid on her by her adoptive families enraged her. The older and prettier she got, the more her sense of self-worth grew, and the more defiant she became of anyone trying to control her.

By the time that she turned 16, she'd had enough. Money had always been the shackle that kept her in her foster homes, and now she'd discovered her own source of income she dropped out of school and moved out, cutting off all contact with foster parents, aunts and uncle, sending her supposedly beloved sisters only sporadic postcards and letters. This was a pattern that would continue throughout her life. She was drawn to her family as the only people who'd ever truly cared for her but repulsed by them in equal measure for the associations they provoked. It was harder to maintain her lies in the face of the people who'd actually been there, and it was easier on Dorothea's nerves to replace her real siblings with the many faces she'd imagined for her Mexican family.

This far south, surrounded by the real Mexican community, it was obvious to everyone that she was a white girl playing at a Hispanic ancestry, so to make her lies easier to swallow, she turned her eyes north. With the little money she'd saved up, she caught a bus up to Washington State, coming to a halt in the state capital of Olympia, where she promptly ran out of cash.

Sharing a tiny motel room overlooking the Puget Sound with another teenaged girl, that she met at the bus station, Dorothea set out to make herself a nest egg and get herself established in this new and exciting place. At 16, her smooth skin, blue eyes and silky pale hair made her the picture of beauty for the time. Combined with her lightly affected Mexican accent, she became exotic too. In no time at all, she was securing customers, following in her mother's footsteps, but almost immediately surpassing her in terms of earnings.

The year 1945 was a good time to be a prostitute in the United States. The Second World War was coming to an end, and a flood of soldiers was returning from around the globe. Many of them had not seen a woman in many years, and even the ones that had craved the familiar comfort a girl like Dorothea could offer. She had to take on a second motel room to accommodate the sheer number of visitors that she and her new friend from the bus station were fielding, and even then, there weren't enough hours in the day for her to entertain her guests. Among the men paying to have sex with the teenage girl was Fred McFaul, a 22-year-old soldier who'd just returned from a bloody deployment in the Pacific. He became infatuated with Dorothea during his visits, booking not just the regular slot but also extra time just to talk with her. She shared her story of life in Mexico, peppered with sadness about her tragically dead parents, intended to elicit sympathy. The besotted McFaul was entirely taken in by the blatant and often clumsily constructed falsehoods that she'd spun and saw the way that she was living as a sign of her fall from grace rather than a deliberate descent into the gutter.

Within a few weeks, he proposed marriage to the teenage prostitute, and with no better options on the horizon and her steady stream of customers beginning to dry up as they settled back into civilian life, Dorothea said yes.

The young lovers took their first steps into a relationship, with Dorothea latching onto Fred's pocketbook almost as readily as she did him. She stopped turning tricks once she was certain he'd provide for her, but her tastes ran to the expensive — silk stockings, floral print dresses and constant hair appointments. Her beauty was the only thing she was sure of, and there was no price too high to accentuate it. Now that she'd had a taste of easy money from her hooking days, she was unwilling to go back to any sort of regular life. She wanted the best of everything, and besotted Fred made sure that she got it.

Two months later, they made the long journey south into Nevada and tied the knot in Reno in a ridiculously expensive and over-the-top ceremony. All of Fred's family lived in Nevada, so they attended, and Dorothea was soon spinning her old story about her family back in Mexico and how she couldn't get in touch with any of them. It was one of several conflicting stories that she told to guests on the day, expecting to never be in the same room with most of them ever again, even going so far as to claim that she'd been rescued by Fred from the Bataan Death March during the war in the Philippines — despite the fact that she would've only been 13 at the time. The McFaul family were perplexed, to say the least, but most attributed her tall tales to nerves and champagne rather than anything more malevolent. She was young, after all, and the young were prone to flights of fancy.

After the big event, Fred had secured work for himself in Gardnerville. The honeymoon period was glorious for both of them. Dorothea had finally found someone who cared about her or at least cared about the person that she was so intent on pretending to be. She showed her appreciation for that care in the only way she knew how. By the time that they'd rented a small house in Gardnerville within easy walking distance of his parent's old house, the besotted Fred had moved on to being almost overwhelmed by his wife's constant attention. So overwhelmed that he suspected she'd become a prostitute, not so much out of desperation as out of a need to satisfy her nymphomania.

Sex was not openly discussed in the 40s, but even if it had been, it would have seemed bizarre to the young man that his complaint was too much of it. Luckily, once they had settled into their new home, Dorothea began diverting some of her attention into the kitchen rather than the bedroom. If he'd begun to doubt her Mexican heritage, those doubts were soon washed away by the flavours that soon graced his plate. Even if everything else about growing up in Mexico had been a lie, Dorothea certainly could cook the food, and she cooked it well. The same could not be said for the rest of her housekeeping. Fred was used to military precision, so when he was confronted with the mess in his home, he didn't even know how to respond. Dorothea had never been taught, by lesson nor example, how to keep a home in a decent state. Those duties fell to him, even though he complained about them incessantly. Sensing his dissatisfaction, Dorothea redoubled her efforts in the bedroom, but even that just seemed to drive a wedge between them. It was almost a relief when she fell pregnant, and thus, he had an excuse to avoid intimacy.

A year into their marriage, she gave birth to a baby girl. After hours of agonising labour, thanks to a body that was still too young to safely carry a baby to term, Dorothea held that baby in her arms, looked down at it and felt absolutely nothing. It went beyond having no personal examples of good motherhood and into something more sinister at that point. Whatever bond a mother and child should have had, never formed, and so the cycle of abuse by neglect continued to the next generation.

Fred was horrified to come home from work and find the house was not only a mess, as always, but that the baby had been left to crawl amongst the filth, wrapped in the same reeking nappy it'd been wearing when he left in the morning. Three months after their first daughter was born, Dorothea dumped the baby on her mother-in-law.

Once again confronted undeniably by his wife's shortcomings, Fred grew more distant. It was obvious to him that something had gone seriously wrong during the pregnancy and birth that had resulted in Dorothea's complete lack of interest in her child, but he couldn't explain it in any terms that made sense when his mother demanded that she come and fetch the baby back. He didn't like to confront Dorothea about anything in case her temper flared up and she went off drinking, as she had the first time they'd had an argument. He didn't like to see Dorothea drunk and angry any more than he liked the rumours that trickled back to him about her showing altogether too much interest in other men when she was out on those benders.

With Fred gone much of the time and nothing much to do, Dorothea found herself bored. She started to buy in a little liquor to soften the sharp edges of that boredom, but that just made her moods even more volatile and Fred more distant. She didn't fall immediately into the arms of other men, although she was still turning plenty of heads in town, but neither one of them felt like their needs were being met.

Gradually, she began to clean up her act and make the house more liveable, but it was primarily out of a desire to fill the hours of her days rather than because she felt any great desire for cleanliness. Even so, Fred saw this as an attempt at reconciliation, and he tried to meet Dorothea half-way. As with most of their reconciliations, this took place primarily in the bedroom.

Sex and alcohol filled the void inside Dorothea that a normal person might have filled with love and affection. If sensations were all that she could feel, then she would set out to feel them as often as possible. Fred mistook that lust for love, as he had from the start, so when it turned out that she was pregnant once more, he believed that it would be the turning point in their relationship — that she would bond properly with their second child and they could settle into a normal life, maybe even bring their firstborn home to share in the new life they were building.

Dorothea went into labour while he was at work and quietly took herself to the hospital without a single word to anyone — not that any of her husband's family in Nevada were still talking to her. This second childbirth was less painful, and Dorothea came out of it with considerably more wherewithal than she had the first. Before the baby had even been latched onto her breast, she was already making enquiries about adoption.

She arrived home the next day with no baby and no bump. Fred was understandably confused, and in her later years, Dorothea would no doubt have spun some tragic tale about a bloody miscarriage to extract the maximum amount of sympathy from her husband. As it was, she was tired of him and tired of her life in Gardnerville. When he confronted her about the missing baby, she told him the truth. She didn't want it, so she'd given it up.

Fred rushed around, making a fuss to the relevant authorities, but his new daughter was already long gone, with all parental rights signed away. It was the last straw. His next stop was to collect divorce papers, and Dorothea didn't trouble to contest it. Instead, she gathered up whatever cash was lying around the house, packed up her cases, and caught the first train to Los Angeles.

The year was 1948, she was freshly divorced at a time where such things were still practically unheard of, and she had no prospects. It was hardly surprising that when people asked what had become of her husband, she spun a story about a brave war hero who died tragically young of a heart attack.

Of Fred and her eldest daughter, very little is known. They didn't stay in touch with Dorothea, even before news of her more horrific exploits came to light. Once more, she was alone in the world.

Cheques and Balances

With a little money in her pocket, Dorothea rented a small apartment in a bad part of Los Angeles, fully expecting to pick up her career as a prostitute from where she'd left off, in a much busier city with considerably more traffic. Unfortunately, 1948 was not as good a year for prostitution as 1945 had been, with everyone working diligently to settle back into their post-war lives. More pressingly for Dorothea, at the age of 19, after birthing two babies and eating like only those who grew up with no access to food could, she found that she couldn't draw in men the way she used to. She wasn't unattractive by any stretch of the imagination, and she was now settling into her assumed Mexican accent more comfortably, but she had lived a hard life, and it was rapidly catching up to her.

By the start of the next year, to supplement her dwindling takings as a prostitute, she began stealing from her clients when she followed them home from the bars of LA. If she could avoid sleeping with her clients and exposing herself to the entailed risks, she would simply slip their cheque books from their pockets while they were fumbling with her over her dress. If she did make it as far as their homes, she would ply them with as much liquor as possible to avoid sex, or to ensure they passed out as quickly as possible afterwards so that she could ransack the place for any cash, cheques or valuables lying around.

Her success as a thief was comparable to her success as a prostitute — a run of extremely good luck and timing that ran out almost as soon as it had started. In early 1949, the police began to receive reports from bemused bartenders about a young woman who was doing the rounds, robbing Johns and writing bad cheques. Sitting in a bar getting hit on by young women was the kind of duty that almost every man of the LAPD was quick to volunteer for, and within a week of the first report coming in, Dorothea was arrested for fraud, if not the initial thefts. With her being so young, the judge was fairly lenient — she was sentenced to a year in prison with the possibility of parole after six months. It was still a terrible shock to the system for the girl, who was, for all her airs and graces, still only 19 years old.

Prison conveyed to Dorothea what a whole marriage to Fred McFaul had failed to drum in. The first time that her cell was allowed to degenerate into filth, she was written up and punished. Worse yet, her fellow prisoners looked down their noses at her in contempt. These women, upon whom Dorothea looked as little better than dirt, treated her as if she were less than them because of her lack of cleanliness. It was the shock that she needed to change her attitude. From that moment on, her cell was the best kept in the whole prison. She had no interest in being a better person, but the thought of being perceived as less than others was enough to spur her into action.

Since leaving her family, Dorothea had very deliberately isolated herself from the society around her. She had no friends, and her interactions outside of her husband and his immediate family were limited to the practicalities. In prison, she began to realise the potential of relationships, both as a means of getting what she wanted and as a source of ego affirmation. In the face of mounting evidence that her looks were rapidly fading, she now found that she could instead allocate value to herself based on the number of people who liked her. Of course, the people with whom she was forming these relationships were often hardened criminals, many of whom were just as manipulative as Dorothea herself, lacking her natural absence of empathy but experienced in the art of deception. Still, she spun the same old lies, refining and perfecting them with time until the whole story of her journey from Mexico to the Philippines, the rescue from the Death March by a valiant young soldier and his tragic heart attack only days after they made it home and were wed was more real to her than her own true history.

While she was in prison, she received the beginnings of an informal education in crime. She practised picking pockets in communal spaces, and during the long hours when she was confined to her cell, she practised forging the different signatures that her new friends had scribbled down for her. More importantly, she was taught to avoid repeating the same patterns from the tales of arrest that came to her from every quarter. The truth was that the police preferred not to arrest women if they could avoid it, and only when they were forced into it by flagrant criminality would they take the necessary steps. If she could remain out of sight, change up her robberies to hit different locations and continue preying on men, who were, in the eyes of the police, little more than criminals themselves, then she could get off with exactly the same crimes she'd already been charged with, forever.

When she emerged from prison four months later, the simple mistakes that she had made the first time around would never be repeated. With fresh knowledge under her belt about the best ways to ply her various trades, Dorothea hit the streets and set about clawing her way back to the level of wealth and comfort that she'd become accustomed to in married life. Some of LA's most successful prostitutes had given her a crash course in the best stretches of road to pick up custom, the low rent motels that didn't bother with a hotel detective and let you linger in the lobby until a man came along looking for trade, and even the names and descriptions of the good, bad and weird clients that might come her way.

She relocated herself from Riverside County to the city centre, which was in direct violation of her parole, and set to work. She no longer needed to rob her clients to make ends meet, and the police were more than willing to turn their eyes away from a little bit of prostitution, particularly when many prominent members of the force made use of their services. She did steady trade, enough for any other woman to comfortably establish herself in the city. But, it was never enough for Dorothea, who immediately spent all of her takings on extravagances: the finest liqueurs, silk stockings, new dresses, new hats and meals eaten out every night. She soon developed stable, regular clients in addition to passing trade. There was a certain amount of repetition in her nightly activities, but before the lights were dimmed, she had the kind of exciting, chaotic life that she seemed to crave.

She probably would've gone on in that manner until the last of her beauty faded and she had to find gainful employment elsewhere if it weren't for the pregnancy. With no access to a safe abortion and no way to maintain her lifestyle with a bastard in her belly, she was forced to abandon prostitution, at least in the short term. She sought out family members and old foster parents to stay with, mooching as much as she could before being bounced along to the next. Her third child came to term in 1950, and she gave birth in a San Francisco hospital. No name was given as to the father on the birth certificate, and when she was asked about the parentage of the baby girl by the adoption agency, she said it was 'just some man.' She hadn't bothered to learn his name, any more than she'd considered the consequences of taking the extra dollar from him in exchange for having sex with him without a condom.

Unknown in San Francisco, she had a much easier time of circumventing local law enforcement, returning to prostitution nominally but earning the majority of her spending money through theft and cheque fraud once again. The experience of her third pregnancy and her dependence on the kindness of others for her own survival had shaken Dorothea. She didn't want to end up in the same situation ever again, so she set out to find economic stability once more through the only means that she had at her disposal.

Husband hunting was harder for an older girl who had been through the ravages of childbirth, life on the streets and prison. Dorothea's love for cookery and her long bouts of near starvation as a child had left her with a propensity for overeating, and she was no longer the lithe, young blonde turning everyone's heads. It would take her almost two years before she could find a new husband.

The Golden Years

Axel Johansson was a merchant seaman of Swedish descent, who was looking to put down roots in San Francisco and make a life for himself on land. He brought in a respectable wage for his work at sea, and he was rarely around to see how that money might be spent — Dorothea's ideal man.

Their courtship was relatively long by the young woman's standards. With Axel being called back to duty so regularly, she barely had the time to get her hooks into him before he vanished once again. Still, he came looking for her each time he made dock, excited to hear more of her stories and to learn of the dramas of her life that he was so envious of.

Dorothea's lies had not stopped for even a moment throughout the years. She wasn't going to share her criminal history with this man while she was still trying to snare him, so she had to come up with some sort of job for herself to explain away her survival. He lapped up the stories of her youth in Mexico and was silenced with sorrow by the tale of her brave soldier husband struck down in his prime. It was reasonable, then, to assume that he would swallow whatever fresh pack of lies she offered him hook, line and sinker.

Her story was straight until 1948, when her husband 'died', so it was there that she laid the groundwork for the rest of her invented past. In a department store named The Emporium, in San Francisco, the 19-year-old Dorothea had been approached by a strange man, who sized her up — hardly an uncommon occurrence for her in those days. But, instead of asking her out on a date, this man had pressed his card into her hands. He was a talent scout for the Radio City Rockettes, the famous New York City dance troupe, and he wanted her to join them. Despite having no training in dance, she had taken fate by the horns and jumped on the first flight out East to compete in auditions. And, wouldn't you know it, her natural grace and talent had been enough to get her through. She was a Rockette! Even still, she wasn't ready to abandon her career in San Francisco, working as the chef in one of the town's top seafood restaurants. She would commute back and forth, working Thursday to Sunday on the stages of New York as Sharon Neyaarda, then flying back to run her award-winning kitchen for the rest of the time.

The seafood aspect was clearly tailored to her assumptions about what sailors might enjoy eating, and having had a few of Dorothea's home-cooked meals by this point in their relationship, Axel could easily believe that the woman was capable of being a chef. On top of all the other momentous events in her life, some of the details that she used to embroider her life story seemed a little preposterous, but she told the stories with such surety and fervour that it was impossible to doubt her.

Her career as a Rockette was brought to a tragic end only shortly before she met Axel, although the date tended to drift slightly in later retellings. Dancing on the stage in front of another full house, Dorothea had been the unfortunate victim of random chance once more. The girl dancing beside her snapped one of her high heels, stumbled into Dorothea and knocked the pair of them into the orchestra pit. While Dorothea escaped the accident with nothing but a broken leg and an ended career, she delighted in furnishing Axel with all of the horrid details of the fate of the other dancer, who was left paralyzed by the accident. Insult was added to injury when she was abandoned to rot in some hospital soaking in her own urine while her husband ran off with another Rockette.

Axel took all of this at face value, taking care never to mention dancing in front of Dorothea in case it hurt her feelings, and proposed to her soon after being introduced to the vast overlapping melodramas that composed her life. Her energy was infectious, even if it came from a place of nervous deception rather than animal magnetism, but that energy in itself was enough to draw him further in. Most of the women he met were put off by his coarse manners and gruff appearance. To find one that seemed not only genuinely interested in him but also fascinating in her own right was a big boost to his bruised ego.

Once they were married in a far more elaborate ceremony than was really required for the incredibly small wedding party, Axel and Dorothea settled into a home on the edge of, what would one day become, suburbia. As with her first husband, Dorothea lavished her attentions, both culinary and sexual, on Axel, making sure before he went off to sea for the first time as a married man that he would not stray.

Left alone in the house for weeks at a time, Dorothea should've been in heaven. This was exactly what she wanted: peace, and the money to do whatever she wanted with that peace. But still, that same burning wanderlust seemed to take over her whenever she sat still for too long. Born into chaos, she would always be restless. In those early days, she drank more than she ate, spending as much time in a drunken haze as she could afford, and her lack of attention soon became apparent by the state of her home. It slid into disrepair rapidly, with Dorothea fully intending to give it one solid tidy before Axel came home from sea. She lost track of the days as she slumped further into alcoholism, and Axel came home to a wreck of a house and a wife passed out in their marriage bed.

In those days, domestic abuse was not spoken about. If a woman's husband had to strike her to reinforce a lesson that he was trying to convey, then the shame was conveyed not onto the violent man but onto the woman for failing to complete her duties how they should've have been. The war changed many things, and women's liberation movements were on the rise by the 50s, but the presiding view was still that a wife was the subject of her husband, not his equal.

She was beaten soundly for her slovenly behaviour, for her drunkenness and for the poor welcome that she offered her husband. The punitive measures seemed to work — she immediately cleaned up her act. By the time that the bruises had faded, their home was as pristine as the day he'd first set sail; there was a delicious meal on the table each night, and their evenings were spent in intense conversation. More and more ridiculous details were added to Dorothea's stories on those evenings. She regaled Axel with stories about her time with the Rockettes and the star-studded lifestyle that she'd led before abandoning it all to settle down with him. John Kennedy, the future president, was appearing more and more often in the news, so he and his wife Jackie were woven into her tales. The actress Rita Hayworth was cast as Dorothea's best friend, and she could spend hours spinning tales about their times together in New York, mostly harvested from the gossip columns of newspapers. The longer that Axel spent in her company, the more he seemed to grow tired of her, and the more extravagant her inventions became. Eventually, she began tripping over her own stories, trying to keep him enthralled with the image of her as a glamorous creature, but the more that she pushed the limits of credulity, the more he withdrew from her.

He dreaded what he would find if he went back out to sea again and delayed returning to work for as long as he could, but as their savings dwindled, he was forced to leave Dorothea behind once more. Once again, the same pattern repeated: boredom, liquor and a gradual decline. Dorothea started trawling bars for the attention she felt she lacked at home, and she found it in spades. Her body had thickened over the years, but she still knew just how to dress to emphasise her best assets, and the stories that'd made her husband so confused were lapped up by the men that she pressed up against in bars. Over the years that followed, Dorothea would often bring men home and sleep with them in her marriage bed. Taxis would appear late in the evening, delivering strange men to her parlour. The neighbours never accused her outright of prostitution, or anything so coarse, but they did see to it that news of her infidelity made it back to Axel when he came back into town.

The beatings grew in their regularity over the years of their marriage, but even at her most bruised and battered, Dorothea never blamed her husband for his actions. She was the one who was creating the problem; he was merely trying to correct it. Over and over through their marriage, this same pattern repeated. Dorothea's stories became more extravagant, her behaviour more erratic.

When asked by the neighbours about her life before moving to San Francisco, she would tell a garbled mixture of the tales she'd made up for Axel and new ones that she'd created for the men in bars, alcohol muddling her memory and ability to keep her stories straight. Some of them she told about her career in the Rockettes, but while half of them heard about her tragic fall into the orchestra pit, the others heard about how Rita Hayworth had taken her back to Hollywood and made her a star in the pictures. When asked what roles she'd played, she would reply, 'the evil woman', a starring role in dozens of pictures that nobody had ever heard of. The strangest, and perhaps most ominous, story that she told anyone who might ask was about her current career — she claimed to be a 'holistic doctor'. Visitors to her home couldn't deny that she had an interest in medicine — there were a plethora of drug bottles about and books documenting the effects of different medicines were left scattered over every surface. Many people in the neighbourhood would come to her for advice when they took ill as a result, and she soon found herself being drawn into the community almost against her will.

For a time, Axel took this as a good sign — a sign that his wife was finally settling into a normal life with friends and ties to the community — but as her obsession progressed and she began prescribing treatments and medicines to people, often furnishing them with drugs that she'd acquired herself, he became increasingly nervous. Even in her wildest fantasies, Dorothea had never mentioned any time spent in medical school, and he became more and more convinced that she was going to kill someone with the pills she was handing out like candy. When he tried to confront her about it, Dorothea switched her story yet again, talking about the medical training that she'd received back in Mexico and how she'd travelled around remote villages dispensing medicine alongside her beloved mother. It was the last straw for Axel. Before, he had been able to discount Dorothea's conflicting stories as mistakes or failings of memory, but this was a wholesale rewriting of history. It made him realise just how little he knew about his wife, and how much trust he had put in her word. Before the situation could escalate further, he took what he considered to be the necessary steps to ensure Dorothea and the neighbourhood's safety. In 1961, he had her committed.

Dorothea did not have a pleasant stay in the San Francisco Marine Hospital. There was no distinction between the criminally insane and members of the public who were currently undergoing a crisis. The hospital was also shared with sick sailors carrying all manner of horrific diseases from around the world. The administration of the hospital also left a lot to be desired, and it was only when Axel directly intervened on her behalf that Dorothea was taken off the schedule to be surgically sterilised in the eugenics program that was still in operation there.

For their part, the doctors found Dorothea, with her constantly changing stories and her pleas for sympathy, to be a very confusing patient. Mental healthcare was still in its infancy in the 50s, and Dorothea's diagnosis today would've been wildly different. Narcissism and psychopathy were both recognised as symptoms rather than as underlying conditions in themselves, so Dorothea's manipulative stories and utter lack of empathy were taken to be the result of undifferentiated schizophrenia. They believed that she couldn't distinguish between her 'realistic hallucinations' and real events, and this was what caused her to have no emotional attachment to those around her. She was ordered to give up alcohol, which was thought to exacerbate the symptoms of schizophrenia, and then handed back into her husband's tender loving care.

Axel didn't know what to do with her. He couldn't stay at home and watch her every hour of the day — he had to go to sea for weeks or months at a time. And even with his presence, Dorothea seemed reluctant to change. She'd considered all of his previous punishments to be just, a fair response to her failings as a wife, but she didn't take kindly to her confinement in the state mental hospital.

The void between them grew wider and wider with each passing day. Dorothea was kept sequestered in their home. Her only contact with the world outside was Axel, and even he was reluctant to speak to her most of the time. The stigma attached to mental illness now is nothing compared to the shame connected with it in the 60s. Axel had taken pains to ensure that nobody knew where Dorothea had gone when she was in the hospital, implying that she was visiting with relatives. But, now that she was back home, he found it difficult to continue manufacturing excuses. Eventually, the time came for him to return to work, and so given no other option, he handed Dorothea back her freedom and walked away.

Throughout the entire journey, he dreaded what he would come back to and what fresh chaos Dorothea might've invited into his house. There had been times when he was certain she'd had a man staying with her, other times when it seemed she'd thrown raucous parties. Who knew what she might do now? He spent his whole time at sea consumed with dread and rushed home the moment that he got into port. As it turned out, he shouldn't have worried. The place was spotlessly clean, meticulously organised and carefully locked up. The only thing that was missing was his wife. She had vanished without a trace.

Women's Work

Dorothea fled to Sacramento the moment that Axel's back was turned, scraping together what was left of their savings as cash and heading for fresh pastures. While she'd lost the body that had made her such a hit as a prostitute, she still had all of the business acumen that had let her excel in criminal enterprises. She got in touch with some of the local girls and put her organisational skills to work, setting them all up in a house where clients could come and go at all hours of the day and receive the kind of service that they were accustomed to — the exact kind of service that she'd been providing out of her family home while Axel was away. The early 60s were another good time to be a prostitute, with all of the social pressures that eventually led to the counterculture driving 'upstanding citizens' into dangerous territory in search of escape. Unfortunately, the success of Dorothea's new venture soon provoked some jealousy from the women whom she'd not taken under her wing, and they reported the location of the brothel to the police.

Normally, this sort of thing would have been overlooked, but the den of sin just so happened to have been set up in Fulton Street, a relatively nice neighbourhood chosen specifically because Dorothea knew that it was less likely to be identified than in a rougher area. Between the location and the tip making the whole operation into an easy win for the Sacramento police, there was enough to spur them into action. An undercover detective entered the building through the bookkeeping operation out front, in the guise of a trucker, and Dorothea explained the pricing and respective virtues of the girls at her disposal. When none of them seemed to be taking his fancy, she offered to fellate him for a discount price. Arrested on the spot, along with the rest of her girls, Dorothea was dragged to the nearest police station, where she was questioned for hours about the operation she'd set up. Throughout all of the questioning, her court appearances, private counsel with a state-appointed lawyer and the rest of her life, Dorothea insisted that she'd not been working as a prostitute or madam of the brothel at all, in direct contradiction to all evidence. According to Dorothea, she was merely visiting a friend, who happened to live in the building when the policeman arrested her. Unsurprisingly, this did not hold up in court. Dorothea was sentenced to 90 days in jail for prostitution and given a pass on the criminal conspiracy charges since it was her 'first offence' as far as the court knew. Her return to jail was a comfort to Dorothea. All of her worst instincts were repressed by an institutional environment, she was forced into a routine, and her alcohol abuse became impossible. All of the symptoms of her 'schizophrenia' were abated by the circumstances, and while she still told wild stories to her fellow prisoners, she was at least able to keep them all straight in the retellings. It was during this month-and-a-half-long sentence that she set her imagined history in stone and began planning her next moves.

She could not be released from Sacramento Prison without providing the state with a fixed address, and all of her calls to Axel had gone unanswered. He was actually in the midst of organising divorce proceedings against her at the time and had been advised not to respond to her in case she caught wind of the legal action. So, at the end of her 90 days in jail, she was arrested immediately for vagrancy and put back into the system to serve another 90 days.

She had honestly expected Axel to drop everything and come pick her up so she could resume her life with him and use him as a springboard to her next set of plans. They'd been married for more than a decade by this point, and despite his violence and regular attempts to set her right, Dorothea genuinely believed that he was still the love-drunk boy she'd picked up in a bar. She thought he was still wrapped around her finger, the perfect back-up plan when her other schemes went wrong. Now she discovered that she had to navigate life without that safety net. With that in mind, she used her time in prison more profitably. It was now obvious to her that she needed some sort of structure to her life or she'd risk running entirely off the rails. It was equally obvious that she needed some steady, legitimate income so that she didn't end up in the same dire straits again.

She'd made a reputation for herself in the prison as a health expert, having memorised drug information and lists of diseases during her 'holistic doctor' phase. She'd originally started down that particular rabbit hole of information when seeking a new ailment to claim that she was suffering from, learning throughout her marriages to date that sympathy was very easy to elicit if you were unwell, and so she would browse through medical dictionaries like another woman might browse a clothing catalogue. She managed to impress everyone with her knowledge, and when her second sentence was over, some of her new friends put her in touch with their friends in the care industry.

Employed as a nurse's aide, Dorothea attended the private homes of the elderly and disabled to help them with activities that they were no longer capable of, administer their medication and keep them company. It was boring work, even for someone with an imagination as active as Dorothea's, and the pay was a pittance compared to what she used to rake in for doing little more than lying on her back and smiling. Still, it didn't take Dorothea long before she began to recognise the potential perks of the job. Instead of buying food herself, she would cook for herself along with her clients. Technically, she was stealing their food, but most of them appreciated the company so much that it didn't even occur to them to object. Similarly, if some of their medication went missing in the process of Dorothea 'tidying the place up', they were rarely troubled by it, as the doctor was always ready to prescribe and deliver more. Soon, sharing food progressed to Dorothea dipping into the client's liquor cabinets to keep herself entertained during the long boring hours when she was meant to be seeing to their needs. In Dorothea's mind, there was only a tiny step from the clients willingly sharing their food to giving her the money to go out and buy food for herself, so if she pocketed any cash that was left lying out while she was cleaning the house, it was hardly any more of an imposition.

Throughout it all, she maintained such a cheerful, friendly outlook that none of her clients suspected a thing was awry. They trusted Dorothea completely, and she repaid that trust by robbing them blind at every turn. When their social security or pension cheques came through, they trusted her to bank them. When they needed money withdrawn from their account to pay for anything, it was Dorothea whom they sent out with their pocketbooks. She was careful about how much she took, and who she took it from, targeting the most vulnerable and confused of her clients for the worst of her avarice.

Surrounded at all times by sickness, Dorothea began developing her own tales of woe to try to elicit sympathy from the social workers she sometimes crossed paths with. She wanted what the dying and disabled had — an endless font of empathy from everyone that she met — but her desire outstripped her intelligence. First, she would complain of breast cancer, then of a brain tumour, then cancer of the liver. Her story switched so frequently that she would often tell the same person different versions on the same day if they met in different houses. Nobody believed her lies, but they considered her odd bouts of hypochondria to be a minor inconvenience given the quality of care that she offered. A health obsession was hardly uncommon among those in the healthcare industry, so she barely even raised an eyebrow.

It was during this period in the early 60s that Axel successfully acquired his divorce from Dorothea, though it seems likely that she wouldn't find out about it for several years to come. Dorothea never removed him from her personalised version of history. Even after the divorce had gone through, she still looked upon Axel kindly, inflating his importance in each retelling, often making him the Swedish Ambassador in her tales, although eventually settling on the story that he was the brother of the famous boxer, Ingemar Johansson.

These years also marked the first time that Dorothea's theoretical knowledge of medicine began seeing some practical applications, not in any official capacity, of course — she would never have been legally allowed to prescribe medicine — but in her capacity as a thief from the elderly. Using the medication found in their own homes, Dorothea doped her clients so that they didn't notice her spending a day lounging around, or so that they would be too dazed to object as she robbed them. When she couldn't trick them into taking extra pills on top of their usual medication, she would grind them up and put them into the food and cocktails that she served, trusting in the spices of her Mexican cuisine or the sharpness of the alcohol to conceal any odd flavours.

More than skill, luck kept Dorothea's clients alive and well, until 1966, when she finally retired from private nursing before the families of some of her clients were able to connect the dots. Even when a few of her clients had died and autopsies were performed, the medication that showed up in their bloodwork was all prescribed to them by a doctor.

Dorothea was careful, unexpectedly wealthy and painfully lonely. She longed for companionship beyond the late-night back-alley fumbling she'd been able to find outside the bars of Sacramento, and she longed for the feeling of community that she'd begun to cultivate when she was married to Axel, a place where she could get all the benefits of being in prison with the comforts of a home. She wanted to be more than just the figure in the background of other people's stories. She wanted the limelight again. With the substantial cash that she'd accrued, she was able to rent a large house on the corner of 21st and F Street. While she knew that an application for a boarding house license would be denied to her, on the basis of her convictions for soliciting, a boarding house was the next natural step in her career as a professional carer — a way for her to parlay the work that she was doing for individuals into something larger and much more profitable.

The passing years had been hard for Dorothea. She had aged badly, easily mistaken for a woman of 50 or 60 by the time she was approaching 40. Even if she could go back to working as a travelling nurse's aide, she didn't really have the energy anymore.

Keeping all of her clients under one roof would let her care for far more of them simultaneously while also giving her the opportunity to steal any money that came in for them at its source. The only trouble was, that same exhaustion prevented her from doing the vital work that was required to get the house ready for guests. She needed an able-bodied, younger man to do the heavy lifting and physical labour for her, a man who came cheap since her savings were already dwindling after putting down her deposit on the place. She tried to recruit the local homeless population but found they were almost all too unreliable, preferring to wander off the moment they'd been paid for a day's work and unwilling to work if money wasn't forthcoming on that first day.

Eventually, help came from the most unexpected of places. In her ongoing attempts to slip back into some role within society, Dorothea had been contacting the local Hispanic community, pretending to have Mexican ancestry and spinning her usual webs of lies. Her carefully calculated story touched the hearts of many, and so when it became known that she was struggling to get the work on her boarding house completed so that she could take care of the elderly of the city, everyone jumped to her aid. There was a small but growing population of illegal immigrants in the city of Sacramento, who were in desperate need of some cash-in-hand work, and they showed up in great numbers to help Dorothea achieve her dreams. But, one of those young, lost men set his eyes on her and started dreaming of his own future.

Marriages and Empty Rooms

Roberto Puente was a Mexican immigrant aged only 20 years old when he 'fell' for Dorothea. In her, he saw a future for himself in the United States, a life where he did not have to hide from the immigration authorities, and where he didn't have to work all hours of the day for a pittance just to put food on the table. Dorothea had money — that much was obvious from the fancy clothes she wore and the airs and graces that she affected. More importantly, he'd seen her looking at him and understood exactly what those burning stares meant. When someone was letting their heart rule them, they could ignore any of the silly little worries that the head provided. She wouldn't even question why a man young enough to be her son wanted to take her to bed, or down the aisle.

Their relationship soon developed beyond business, and all of the other illegal workers were let go. He would be the full-time handyman for the boarding house, and she would provide for him in whatever way he desired. They made an odd couple, with her hair already starting to turn white and his head already turning whenever a girl went by.

The boarding house opened in late 1966, and almost immediately all two dozen of the rooms were filled up. The state had an overwhelming number of disabled and homeless people in its care, and the social workers who saw Dorothea providing her residents with clean clothes and home-cooked meals every day considered her to be something like a saint. They didn't give a damn that her boarding house was unlicensed when she did so much for the community. The actual extent of her hospitality was fairly minimal compared to any real establishment, but it was so far beyond what the homeless and chronically ill residents were accustomed to that they sang her praises at every opportunity. And if the odd cheque went missing in the mail, then that was just a part of life with an ever-fluctuating address.

In 1968, Dorothea and Roberto travelled to Mexico City, where they had an extravagant wedding; the third largest in Dorothea's life. She adored it in Mexico, claiming that she was home at last, despite never having even visited before. She was quite reluctant to return to the drudgery of tending to the elderly and the sick, or to her ongoing suspicions that Roberto's wandering eye may have become something more sinister.

With his citizenship assured, Roberto's fidelity began to wane. He endured Dorothea's lustful honeymooning for as long as he could stomach before moving into one of the spare rooms in the boarding house, complaining of her snoring. He was never quite stupid enough to bring another woman back there, knowing that the residents were thoroughly in Dorothea's thrall and ready to report on his activities at the drop of a hat, but it was still the first step away from conjugal life and into something more exciting. As she was a pillar of the community, respected by all, stories filtered back to Dorothea about sightings of Roberto in the company of other women. He was openly courting several girls his own age when he first met Dorothea years before, and that had never stopped, but just became more subtle. He was lying to all of them, insisting to each of his women that the others either didn't exist or that they meant nothing to him. He was a wannabe Lothario of the worst sort, and it was only luck and his growing disgust at his plump, elderly wife that protected her from any number of sexually transmitted diseases. Still, Dorothea found herself untroubled by what her young husband did behind closed doors so long as he presented a good face for the Hispanic community and the many opportunities that Dorothea was finding there.

Sacramento was a city in the grip of innumerable social gripes in the late 60s, from homelessness and drug abuse to the new and pressing concern of the de-institutionalisation of the majority of the mentally ill people in the country from the now-reviled state hospitals that had once kept them contained. While this massive political movement had allowed patients to escape atrocious conditions, it had also left them without any means of accessing treatment, abandoned in a world that had long ago left them behind. The end result of which was a spate of crimes that followed no logical course and a massive growth in the homeless population that almost approached the population movements of the Dustbowl.

All of these crises called out for cash. Money was the only solution to the nation's sweeping social ills. No matter how much anyone volunteered as Dorothea did, it was generally accepted that major change could not be made without political lobbying, massive charitable programs and reformation of the state hospital system.

Dorothea had always revelled in being the centre of attention, spending every penny that she'd acquired on fancy clothes, makeup, perfume and similar fripperies, but now that her beauty was in decline, she found some other way to invest her cash that gave her just as much, if not more, attention. She became a massive donor to many charities, attended many $50-a-plate banquets, and established herself in the upper classes of Sacramento society as the de facto spokesperson for huge swathes of the Hispanic community through her contributions to many important political war chests. The glamorous life that she'd always invented for herself, full of suave politicians, beautiful starlets and music, was suddenly her reality. She ate dinner with Pat Brown, Ronald Reagan and his first wife, Jane Wyman. Through her connections with Reagan, she began attending more evening events with senators and even, on one memorable occasion, major Republican contributor Clint Eastwood — although she was disappointed to find that he was more interested in his date than her.

All of the money that she was throwing around demanded that she steal more and more from her residents, but the unexpected result of all her schmoozing was that she now had an unexpected air of legitimacy about her. The suspicion that might once have latched onto her as her clients' cheques and personal belongings went missing now slipped right off her. She needed only have one brief conversation with the police, following the first bout of accusations against her, about the kind of clients that she provided housing to, their memory troubles and the way that they often preyed on one another, sometimes unintentionally. On the walls behind her in the little private room that she'd set aside for herself in the boarding house were a massive collage of framed photographs, each one of them of her or her husband shaking hands with a celebrity, politician or other local person of influence. The message was clear: this was a well-connected woman who could be trusted a little bit more than some mentally ill homeless people who thought they'd lost a diamond ring sometime in the last year. Still, the complaints continued to flow in every direction, both from current residents and past ones. Claims that Dorothea was pocketing social security cheques and only paying out spending money to her residents fell on deaf ears in the social work community, where it was considered that anyone putting the brakes on an alcoholic's access to liquor was probably doing the right thing. Throughout all of this, Roberto had been enjoying the benefits of the marriage without doing much of the required work. He'd been spending less and less time at the boarding house as the money flowed more readily, and that became clear as the building began to fall into disrepair. Dorothea eventually had to recruit a few of the more reliable homeless residents of the neighbourhood to do odd jobs for her to keep up appearances for the constant visits from social workers. While he would come along to the fancy dinners and shows that Dorothea attended, it wasn't to be in her company for any longer than was necessary to get to the free food and open bar. The social aspect of their marriage had also deteriorated beyond all repair; they argued incessantly in the small amount of time that they spent together, they'd not shared a bed since the very first days of the marriage and Roberto was ever more open about his disgust of Dorothea. He'd checked out of his marriage in every way that mattered, long before things became more serious with one of his other girls.

By the time that he officially left, it seems that Dorothea had made her peace with it. When she found his room in the boarding house empty, she treated it like any of her other flight-risk tenants vanishing in the middle of the night. She boxed up anything he'd left behind, pocketed anything of value, and gave the room a thorough clean. If anything, her abandonment was a relief for Dorothea. She no longer had to uphold the façade of a marriage on top of the many other duties that filled her days. It also gave her the freedom to start looking for a new husband without any judgement from the community. She had been abandoned, so she firmly held the moral high ground, even if Roberto ever did come back.

Dorothea hit the bars of Sacramento with a bounce in her step. The years may not have treated her kindly enough to attract a young man again, but she had a certain amount of glamour to her thanks to her fine clothes and makeup that reminded older gentlemen of the celebrities of a bygone age. It probably helped that Dorothea seemed to have developed a newfound interest in the older man, an interest that often manifested during her barroom conversations with them when she enquired at great length about which benefits they were receiving from the state. She managed to fill several of her empty boarding house rooms with barflies before becoming more aggressive in pursuing what she really wanted as time went by.

She slipped back into her old routine, with a slightly classier twist. She would allow older gentlemen to invite her home, then rob them blind after the drugs that she'd slipped into their drinks kicked in. A few of them were still conscious but unable to move during her ransacking of their homes, so it wasn't difficult for the police to pull together a description of the mystery robber striking fear into the lonely hearts of embarrassed older men. The police began closing in on her, talking to business owners who'd been handed forged cheques, and bartenders who'd seen their best customers vanish off into the night with a mysterious, glamorous woman only to return with horror stories the next day — far more victims than had been reported to the police, of course.

Of all her victims' tales, one of the most harrowing has to belong to Malcolm McKenzie. He was a 74-year-old pensioner and a regular at the Zebra Club. He had seen her around several times before they finally got together. They had several drinks together, with her gradually gathering information about him under the guise of being interested. Then, when he invited her back to his place, she insisted on getting him one more drink before they departed. On the taxi ride home, Malcolm began to feel dizzy, but he put it down to a long day and the liquor that he'd consumed, rather than anything more insidious. Yet, when they got back to his apartment, he found that he had to lean heavily on Dorothea's shoulder to make it up the stairs. Inside the apartment, she dumped him unceremoniously onto the couch and then stalked off to dig through his belongings in search of anything valuable. Trapped in place by the drugs, he could do nothing as she stole his rare penny collection, his cheque book and all of the cash he had hidden in the house. Finally, she came over to look at him where he lay paralyzed. Despite his terror at what she might do next, his heartbeat was languid thanks to the drugs, and all he could do was watch as she bent down and set to work on his hand. He had a diamond ring on his smallest finger that had caught her attention in the bar, and even though his fingers were swollen, she had no intention of leaving without that prize. After several minutes of tugging on the ring and popping his finger in and out of place, she went to the kitchen to fetch some lard for lubrication. With his finger greased, she was able to work the ring off, and with a pleasing little bounce, she tucked it into her pocket. She leaned in closer with that done, ignoring the injury that she'd done to his aching hand and staring instead into his eyes. He was shaking with the effort of trying to move, but Dorothea did not intend to do him any more damage. Instead, she reached out carefully and drew his eyes shut with her fingertips. He would not recover enough to contact the police about the robbery until the next afternoon, by which time Dorothea had already fenced the stolen coin collection through one of the local homeless men that she was cultivating.

Without propriety keeping her in check, Dorothea was free to continue this way forever, but with every cheque she wrote or wallet she lifted, she came a little closer to being cast into jail once more. It was only luck, and a little lust, that saved her from this fate. In 1976, nine years after her failed, but still legally binding, marriage to Roberto Puente, she met her next 'husband'.

Pedro Montalvo was an alcoholic whom Dorothea had picked up in a bar, intending to make him the latest in the long line of victims she had acquired, but she found herself so charmed by the brash character of the man that she didn't drug his drink. They talked late into the night, and by morning, he'd moved into her little apartment above the boarding house. Her marriage to Roberto may have been short-lived compared to her earlier relationships, but it seemed like it lasted forever in comparison to her time with Pedro.

Once again, the honeymoon period was happy for both partners. They wed in a small ceremony in a local church. Dorothea never tried to file the official paperwork, knowing that her polygamy would show up in the records, and without ever having formally acquired a divorce, she was nervous about the questions that might be posed to her in light of the latest addition to her household. She invited none of her high-society friends, and even from among the Hispanic community, which she wrongly called her own, she brought only a few guests to make everything appear as normal as possible.

This fresh start was already tainted by deception, but it was soon darkened even further when Pedro revealed his rather sinister temper. When Dorothea would not submit to him in all matters without question, he lashed out with his fists, and when he was drunk — which was as often as he could manage — his temper often swung wildly out of control. Dorothea had been hit before by her abusive parents and her first husband, but she'd never been on the receiving end of the kind of beatings that Pedro dealt out for no good reason at all.

Dorothea withdrew from their shared apartment on F Street, spending more and more time in the company of the residents in the boarding house and finding that she actually enjoyed their company and adoration. They were all people on the edge of desperation, and she represented a way for them to hold on to their humanity for a little bit longer. Just as she sheltered them from the outside world, their presence shielded her from Pedro's rages. What had been a parasitic relationship gradually became more symbiotic. She would never have the kind of familial emotional attachment to her boarders that they seemed to crave, but she began to see their value as something more than just a meal ticket.

With his new wife disobedient and absent, his new punching bag perpetually unavailable and his presence clearly an affront to the residents of the boarding house, Pedro did not last long. Just two months after their haphazard wedding, he left Dorothea on a bender that would carry him off across state lines, never to return. If she missed him, it never showed.

With her newfound attachment to the people in her care, Dorothea might've gone from acting like a good person, for the praise and attention, to actually caring about others, if she were capable of such a thing. Instead, she continued to treat them just as badly as she could get away with while still garnering positive attention for her 'kindness'. Still, Pedro did leave her with one positive legacy: she was broken of her desire to have a husband in her life. She could reach out for all of the love and support that she needed from the people in her care, and she had no desire to get chained to another maniac. From this point forward, Dorothea intended to live her life alone, and well.

The Mexican community in Sacramento had already been indebted to Dorothea for the contributions she made to arts and education programs for their advancement, but now, she took a step forward to become something more like a social worker for the women. She used her knowledge of drugs and herbalism to assist them in acquiring birth control, even though the controlling men in their lives forbade it, provided them with advice and even guided some of them through the sticky prospects of divorce proceedings when they were too frightened to stand up to their abusive partners. They called her 'La Doctora', but to many of the women, she was considered to be more of a mother figure, someone who had been through the worst that marriage had to offer and come out the other side brave and unscathed.

She continued to trawl bars, but her methodology changed significantly in light of her new revulsion towards men and the gathering heat around the barroom robberies. Up until now, she had been acting like her younger self, trusting in luck to keep her safe. Now, she started applying some of the criminal skills that she'd picked up during her long prison stays. Rather than robbing the men in the bars, she identified which ones were in receipt of pensions or benefits from the state and then gathered enough information to make a false change of address claim so that all of their future payments were sent to her house on F Street. With so many other cheques of the same kind heading to her house and the constant flux of her clientele, she already had the perfect disguise in place in case any attention was given to these diverted payments.

Between the money that she was drawing from her existing clients and the money she was securing through these acts of treasury fraud, she found that, even with her massive charitable and political contributions, she wasn't spending all of her money each month. She began turning her attention to other potential sources of income — investments that would continue to pay out without her having to put in any additional effort. She was rubbing shoulders with the truly wealthy on a weekly basis, and she'd seen the way that the rich became richer just by letting their money sit in some company. She wanted in, and it was this ceaseless hunt for easy money that brought Dorothea into contact with Ruth Monroe.

One Way Out

As skilled as Dorothea was in the kitchen, it made sense for her to seek out the expertise for her first investment. The fact that she also got to spin her old story about running a seafood restaurant in San Francisco again was just a fringe benefit. Through her connections in the upper crust of Sacramento society, Dorothea was able to track down an up-and-coming catering company that was looking to establish a physical presence for itself on the street — a company started and operated by a woman named Ruth Monroe. The initial investment for the company, and much of the support that Ruth had received during its early years, had come from her husband, but now that he'd taken ill, the business was faltering along with him. Dorothea was like an angel swooping down from on high to invest in the company and get it back on track.

The two of them opened up a food service business together, taking over the food side of the Round Corner Tavern in midtown, continuing to support the lower-income segment of

Sacramento's population with affordable meals, while also pulling in enough money to draw a small wage. Dorothea split her time between the eatery and her other ventures, initially spending a decent amount of time in the kitchen before she grew increasingly bored with the actual work and drifted back to her boarding house. Ruth didn't mind at all. The business was doing well enough to support employees, and the financial backing that Dorothea provided was more than enough of a contribution.

Gradually, the two women became friends, even though Dorothea had no real blueprint for that kind of relationship. Her prison friendships had always been built on necessity and manipulation, her charitable work always had an underlying financial transaction, and her relationships with her residents and the homeless were similarly weighted by a balance of needs and demands, but in Ruth she found someone with whom she wanted to spend time for no reason beyond enjoying her company. Dorothea did not know how to deal with this dynamic, and that made her too uncomfortable to embrace it.

By the spring of 1982, the year after their partnership was formed, the dynamic shifted in more ways than one. Dorothea had been fed information from the police department, warning that her redirected government cheques had been spotted and that evidence was being gathered against her. While there was nothing tying her to the earlier drugging and robberies yet, the men whom she had defrauded of their pensions and disability benefits were much more open with the police, and connections were being made. In light of the allegations against her, the police were now giving some of the theft complaints from her residents a closer look. Without a doubt, they would come up with evidence sooner rather than later that all of the claims against the woman were true. Dorothea had to manufacture a way out of the situation before the police had finished their investigation, or she was headed back to jail, goodwill of the city or no.

Meanwhile, Ruth's life was marred by a fresh tragedy. Her husband's health had taken a turn for the worse, and he had been committed to the hospital for full-time palliative care. He was losing his battle with cancer so badly that the doctors were unwilling to prescribe him anything more aggressive than painkillers. Everyone knew that he was dying and that it was just a matter of time, but nobody could do anything about it. The cost of his care began to take a toll on Ruth, and eventually, she was forced to sell off the family home for a fraction of its worth to ensure that he wouldn't be ejected from his bed. This left her with nowhere to stay and nobody to turn to. Her children lived out of town, and she would've had to give up her whole life, business and any hope of visiting her husband during his final days if she went to stay with them. Without a second thought, Dorothea offered Ruth a room in her apartment above the boarding house. They were partners in business, and there was no reason to think that their excellent relationship wouldn't carry over into a shared home life of similar compatibility.

Ruth was initially surprised at Dorothea opening her home to her but soon accepted readily. She couldn't have been less prepared for the way that she was treated in her business partner's home. It was as though she were royalty. Dorothea went beyond being merely a good hostess, but over the top into a level of kindness and attentiveness that nobody could have expected. Ruth could see why so many people wanted to stay in Dorothea's boarding house if they were all treated this way. To begin with, it was like a dream come true. Then, the sickness struck.

Ruth found herself sluggish in the mornings, too tired to do much of anything throughout the day. Dorothea waited on her hand and foot during those strange bouts of weakness, and Ruth soon found herself indulging in cocktails to calm her nerves, despite spending a lifetime sober. The alcohol took the edge off of her panic at her condition and provided Dorothea and her cocktail shaker with an easy way to administer the drugs that were causing Ruth's illness, to begin with.

In early April, a few weeks after Ruth moved in, William Clausen, her son, came to visit after hearing about her illness, travelling to Sacramento from his home out in South Land Park. He was shocked to find her with a crème de menthe in her hand, giggling away quite happily. She was pallid, too weak to stand and seemingly unconcerned. Dorothea was taking good care of her. She used to be a nurse. They had nothing to worry about. Nothing at all.

The whole situation was suspicious. He'd never even heard of this Dorothea woman until a few weeks ago, and now, suddenly, she was his mother's best friend, providing her with around the clock care? Something didn't add up. But, every time that he tried to talk to Ruth about the situation, Dorothea contrived a reason to be there, watching and waiting, ready with excuses. He was on the receiving end of many of Dorothea's tales during his visit, all of them calculated to paint the white-haired woman as a saint of Sacramento. All of her charitable work, her history as a nurse, her current role as medical adviser to the undocumented immigrants and frightened housewives of the city, they all painted a picture of her as the kind of woman who could be trusted with his mother's life, but something about her blank-eyed stare just didn't fill him with confidence. She could say all of the right words and go through all of the right motions, but the emotion never ran deeper than the surface.

Disturbed and confused, William had to head home to his family at the end of the day, but his suspicions would not abate. He knew, in his gut, that something was wrong with the situation on F Street, but all of the pieces weren't in place yet for him to see the bigger picture.

By the end of April 1982, Ruth was dead, and the police were swarming through the apartment above the guest house. With the other outstanding investigations against Dorothea, she was the natural suspect in her business partner's death, but the interviewing detectives found no trace of the calculating killer that they'd hoped to find. Dorothea seemed distraught at the loss of her friend, devastated at the closure of her business and traumatised by the aggressive questioning that she'd been subjected to. She was hardly anyone's picture of a murderer. The investigating officers wanted to find some other explanation for Ruth's death, and Dorothea delivered it to them gift wrapped.

Ruth's husband was in the hospital, dying, and she'd been profoundly depressed about the whole situation. Depressed and drinking. The coroner discovered a massive overdose of Ruth's prescribed medications in her system, mixed with a cocktail of over-the-counter drugs that would have been readily available to anyone with ready cash. Suicide seemed to be the obvious explanation.

If killing another human being had any effect on Dorothea, then it certainly wasn't visible. She went about the same routines as always, tending to her residents, picking up pensioners and forging their cheques, and processing the necessary paperwork to shut down operations in the Round Corner Tavern and disperse the few employees that they'd managed to hold onto during Ruth's 'illness'. She told everyone and anyone about the tragic suicide of her friend, repeating the same story over and over for sympathy — making it, like so many other lies, into a part of her own life story; the great piecemeal fiction that she used as a shield against the pain of encroaching reality and as a tool to deflect any sense of responsibility for her actions. By the end of the investigation, it's possible that she'd even managed to convince herself that it was the truth. That the pills she'd ground up and mixed into Ruth's drinks weren't nearly enough to kill her, and the painkillers that had been poured down the old woman's neck didn't have the power to take a life. There was a massive disconnect from the actions that she'd taken and the end result, and that was all that she needed to entertain some sort of reasonable doubt. Maybe Ruth had taken more pills. Maybe she had been knocking them back in a genuine suicide attempt every time that Dorothea's back was turned. Surely it was possible that the official version of events was the true one? That she'd watched with tearful eyes as her beloved friend and business partner took her own life? The truth had always been a malleable thing for Dorothea, and now that she was faced with the starkest and most evil thing that she'd ever done, it was hardly surprising that she shied away from the truth on a grand scale. William was not satisfied when the official case was closed. He knew that Dorothea was responsible for his mother's death, even if he didn't know how or why, but it took him weeks of poring over his mother's accounts before he realised the motive behind the killing. Ever since she'd moved into the F Street apartment, transfers had started from her savings account into her business, payments that gradually increased until they were a steady flow, draining away all of the money from the sale of Ruth's home into the joint account that Dorothea also had access to. As the executor of her estate, William could see the money sitting in that joint account, going nowhere, and he was poised to report the theft to the police the very moment that Dorothea tried to withdraw anything. He underestimated Dorothea.

The other investigations into her fraudulent activities were closing in, and the report of a robbery from Malcolm McKenzie had just added more fuel to the fire. Dorothea's informants within the department were falling silent one by one, with her most stalwart supporters trying to direct her to a decent criminal lawyer. None of that was necessary; she had a plan, and now, she had the cash she needed to put it all into motion.

Unfortunately for Dorothea, the police trap snapped shut faster than she'd anticipated. They caught wind of the fact that their prime suspect had booked a plane ticket to Mexico and caught her as she was heading for the taxi with her luggage in tow. All of her plans to start a new life south of the border with Ruth's savings as a nest egg fell apart on contact with the cold reality that she had been caught.

Still, her unexpected move did net some benefits. The 30 or more fraud cases that were being pulled together against her still weren't completely investigated by August when she had her day in court, and the judge, Roger Warren, insisted on discounting them and any previous convictions when the time came to pass sentence on her. He was moved by Dorothea's doddering old mother act and was aware of her connections to the upper echelons of society. Access to celebrities might have vanished the moment that she was arrested, but not all of the benefits of her longstanding contributions evaporated so quickly. She was given the benefit of doubt where nobody else would've been. For the three robberies that she was convicted of, as a result of the few completed investigations, she was to serve five years, and as terms of her parole afterwards, she would no longer be allowed to run a boarding house or work with people of diminished capacity. The elderly, the mentally ill, the disabled, the addicted — all of the people that she'd made her fortune exploiting would be forever out of reach for her as long as she abided by the terms of her parole. This may have just become the latest in a long line of criminal schemes for Dorothea, but over the years, she'd found herself becoming the mask that she'd crafted so diligently. She loved the lifestyle, the celebrity status and the attention that her life as a pillar of the Hispanic community had granted her, and she felt the loss of all that considerably more than the loss of her freedom.

So, instead of settling into a life of comfort and respect as 'La Doctora' in Mexico City, Dorothea now found herself in Sacramento County Jail.

Black Widow

Dorothea was an old hand at prison life by this point, with years of experience under her belt. She made the natural transition from being a young debutante under the wing of the motherly elders of the prison to being in the parental role to the young women of the block, who came around for advice and to listen to her many tales, a few of which were even true. She played up her innocence whenever she was in public, but in private conversations with the younger women, she would let little details slip that might help them in their criminal careers — passing on her wisdom to the next generation in exactly the same way that had been done to her.

She loved to talk so much that she would ignore the usual divisions within the prison, passing through different gangs and racial divides without anyone batting an eyelid. Here, she was well-liked by everyone — right up until the moment that her flapping mouth got her into trouble, three years into her sentence.

Nobody minded Dorothea spreading gossip around the prison. In fact, she was a pretty reliable means of communicating information across the invisible borders within the building. But, there was a massive difference between sharing gossip with other prisoners and talking to the guards. One of them was expected and helpful; the other was tantamount to treason against the natural order of things. When the name of the person responsible for an assault in the prison came to the guards' ears via Dorothea's mouth, the response had to be swift and brutal to make sure that no other prisoners thought it a good way to curry favour and preferable treatment from their oppressors.

Cornered in the showers, Dorothea was beaten within an inch of her life and left to bleed on the tiles. She was transferred first to the hospital wing, where her cracked ribs were wrapped, then moved along into solitary confinement and protective custody until things died down. As it turned out, things wouldn't die down for almost a year. The inter-faction fighting that had prompted the initial assault flared up the moment that punishments were handed down to the perpetrators, and as more and more of the gang leaders were tossed into solitary confinement, so too went the only means of keeping their respective gangs under control. All of this meant nothing to Dorothea, however. All that she knew was boredom and loneliness.

In desperation, she finally turned to the prison pen-pal scheme that she'd always treated with derision before, and through it, she found a sort of revival. In her letters, she could be anyone. She had all the time she needed to plot and plan her exact words and get her story straight before she had to send it off. Every half-fumbled lie that had earned her looks of doubt and confusion could be smoothed into part of a grander story. It was the perfect medium for her to reinvent herself all over again, and with her gift for storytelling, she was a hit with all of her correspondents. One of the men who wrote to her almost daily soon became a favourite and the focus of more and more of her attentions: Everson Gillmouth.

Everson was a retired gentleman currently living in Oregon. He was a widower with several children whom he rarely saw, and he was so intensely lonely that he'd turned to women's prisons in a vain hunt for some sense of companionship. By all accounts, he was a lovely gentleman, with a lot of love to give but absolutely no idea how to go about dating now that he was in his early seventies. He was lost, and in Dorothea, he thought that he'd found a new anchor to the world and new hope for the future. Their early correspondence soon blossomed into friendship, if you can call a one-sided relationship based entirely on deception a 'friendship'. Soon, they were shooting back-and-forth daily replies, and he was dropping cash into her commissary account so that she could keep herself in the manner to which she was accustomed to, for the remainder of her stay.

By the time that Dorothea had been returned to the general population of the prison, and her mail was no longer being so closely monitored, talk had moved on from mere friendship to a more serious relationship, and the two of them made plans for their future together. Everson planned to move to Sacramento so that they could live together, and there was talk about a wedding. It was everything that the young Dorothea, obsessed with being loved and cherished by a husband, would've dreamed of, but Everson arrived too late to find that woman. Instead, he was sending his letters to the woman who'd killed her best friend for the price of a plane ticket. The woman who'd drugged and robbed the men who took an interest in her so that she could stockpile their wealth and maintain her luxurious lifestyle. A cold-hearted, calculating killer.

After three years in prison, Dorothea was released on parole, and Everson was parked outside waiting to collect her in his shiny, red, 1980 Ford pickup. The two of them embraced, she planted a chaste kiss on his lips and they headed off to the rest of their lives together — all three months of it.

The original boarding house on F Street had passed into new hands and was undergoing renovations, but with Everson's wealth behind her as collateral, Dorothea was able to get a new, smaller house and apartment further down the street. The two of them opened a joint account together in preparation for the wedding, and Everson redirected his substantial pension there so that they could start demonstrating their income in advance of mortgaging the new boarding house. They were smiling when they went into the bank together to sign all of their respective papers, but behind her mask of sanity, Dorothea was already making plans to ensure that the pension went on paying forever and that Everson wasn't around to collect it. For all that there were new elements to the scheme, it was much the same as all of her other fraudulent pension thefts. Bank transfers were intercepted rather than cheques, but the mechanics of the rest were the same. The only real difference was that this man wasn't going to disappear, leaving the money to flow, without a little bit of intervention on her part.

Her reputation among the upper crust may have been beyond salvation after her prison term, but the people of Sacramento seemed to remember her fondly, in particular, the social workers, illegal immigrants and homeless addicts who'd so often relied on her charity to make their lives more manageable. First, the local Mexican women started to filter through their door, then the homeless and the alcoholics whom she had helped to survive and thrive before. She'd never lost their trust or their acceptance — every one of them had been on the receiving end of the heavy hand of the law before — and they knew that what was right and what was legal only crossed over on occasion.

Dorothea's confidence grew with each new visitor until her story began to warp in response to their adoration. She was no longer the repentant criminal who'd made a few mistakes while trying to do right by the people of Sacramento. Now, she was a martyr to the unfair legal system that punished those who tried their best to help people in need.

One by one, all of her old friends reappeared, asking favours or offering assistance. Everson was amazed at how beloved Dorothea seemed to be within the community of Sacramento, and Dorothea was amazed, in turn, at how easily the officials of the social work department turned a blind eye to the terms of her parole and began filling her new building up with the lost and forgotten who'd fallen through the cracks of society and into her hands. The homeless population was like a vast ocean of bodies, and like any liquid, it would flow out to fill any space that was made for it. This time around, Dorothea was a little more selective in the people that she took in, but not in the way that other boarding houses selected their clients. She chose the very worst and most hopeless cases to be her residents: the people who were almost guaranteed to vanish within a month and never to return, the alcoholics and drug addicts, the mentally ill and the criminals that everyone else would've turned away at a glance. Again, Everson was amazed at the kindness and charity of his new bride-to-be. He couldn't understand how an upstanding woman like her could have found herself in prison. Reality and the stories that Dorothea spun just didn't add up.

When the truth finally arrived for Everson Gillmouth, he recognised it too late. He'd loved the beautiful lie that Dorothea had woven before his eyes, and when the ugly truth behind it was revealed, he didn't know how to respond. He was laid out in what was meant to be their marriage bed, too weak to move, too sluggish to do much more than moan and groan. Just as Ruth had died, so too went Everson.

The moment of his peaceful death, drifting off into a drug-induced haze, was where the similarity between Dorothea's two crimes abruptly ended. There would be no gentle handling by the police this time around. There was no way that she could get away with handing them a body twice and face no charges, particularly when she was already out on parole. Worse yet, while Ruth's body being filled to bursting with drugs was almost expected, Everson had been in inexplicably good health. An autopsy would reveal that Dorothea was behind Everson's death, which implicated her in Ruth's passing, as well. She couldn't risk the body to be officially processed, which meant that she couldn't allow the body to be found. If Everson's corpse vanished, it would have the additional benefit of his continued legal survival. If the world still believed that Everson was alive, then the money that he was due would continue to be delivered into the joint account that he shared with Dorothea.

With his death, Everson had let out a glut of filth from every orifice, as most people do. The bed was soaked in his vomit, urine and excrement, along with all of the forensic evidence that could be easily used to convict Dorothea of his murder, if it were found. So, in a stroke of genius, Dorothea created her own means of corpse disposal based on her experience as a nurse's aide. She wrapped Everson in the bedclothes like a massive cocoon, then sewed the tainted sheets closed. When that proved insufficient to contain his oozing, she then wrapped the whole thing in plastic sheeting, wrapping layer after layer around the body until nothing but the faint stench of death could escape. Even this was only a temporary solution to the problem, of course. The corpse and its wrappings still had to be transported out of the house, and this was where Dorothea's strength seemed to fail her. She was by no stretch of the imagination the frail elderly woman that she presented herself to society as. By 1985, she was only 56, and her time in prison had left her with quite a robust musculature underneath her concealing modest dresses, but even so, she couldn't carry the dead body of a man out of the house alone. The second phase of her plan tackled that problem.

Through her prison and social work connections, and her ties to the Hispanic community, Dorothea had a direct line to a great many ex-convicts to whom she offered work in exchange for cash payment. They'd served as her personal staff throughout the reconditioning work on the new boarding house, just as they had the first, and many of them expected to find ongoing handyman work around the building after being taken under La Doctora's wing. It was well known that working for her was a ticket to an easier life. She offered very fair payment for work that others wouldn't even give to an ex-convict. She judged each individual on their merits, without any consideration for the crimes of which they were accused, and as long as she was never crossed, she could be the best friend that someone fresh from jail could ever have. There were even rumours that she'd set young men up with a wife if they planned on settling down and making a life for themselves outside of prison. As long as Dorothea was on an ex-convict's side, they were on easy street.

One ex-con who was hoping to adjust to life on the outside in comfort was Ismael Florez. Trained as a carpenter and furniture re-upholsterer before his jail time, he'd expected his skills to earn him pride of place in Dorothea's collection of useful young men, but even he was surprised at her generosity towards him. She wanted some donated wood panelling installed in her upper floor apartment above the main boarding house, and she was willing to pay Ismael considerably more than it was worth to get it done. In exchange for his services, she offered him an almost-new, red Ford pickup truck. She explained to him that her boyfriend had moved out to Hollywood and wouldn't be needing it anymore. Ismael was taken aback and protested that it was far too generous a payment, so Dorothea added a little more work to his load to even the scales. If Ismael would panel her apartment and construct a 6-foot-long storage box for her old books and assist her in transporting those old books to a storage locker across town, then she'd feel like it'd been a fair trade. Even with these extra conditions, it was beyond generous, so Ismael set to work immediately, completing both the panelling and the construction job in record time. He delivered the hand-crafted box to Dorothea after his work was done and drove off with a smile on his face to get some dinner.

By the time that he returned, the box was not only full, but Dorothea had nailed it shut 'so nothing can fall out while we're driving'.

It was a tiny oddity that he didn't think twice about, even as the pair of them wrestled the heavy, musty box down the stairs and onto the back of his pickup. The nailed top saved them a lot of trouble. From there, they took a strange taxi ride, with Dorothea directing every single turn until she abruptly yelled at Ismael to stop at the side of the Garden Highway in Sutter County. She'd changed her mind. Nothing in the box was worth keeping. She just wanted to dispose of it. Perplexed, but unwilling to go against the old woman's wishes, Ismael helped her haul the box off the back of the truck and toss it down the slope towards the river. The area was a common dumping ground for unwanted trash, and once the box was tangled up in the undergrowth, it became almost perfectly camouflaged among the other detritus. With the night's work done, Dorothea seemed almost giddy. She went from sour-faced to chattering all the way home, thanking Ismael profusely and sending him off with a little extra spending money in his pocket for all his help.

It'd been a strange experience, but Ismael didn't have much to base a comparison on. He kept expecting to be called back to the house on F Street to do more work since the old woman had been so delighted with him, but it was as though he'd been cut off cold. He replayed the evening over and over in his head, trying to come up with some way that he might have given offence, but he couldn't think of a thing that he'd done wrong. Eventually, he convinced himself that Dorothea had already given him more charity than she could really afford and that now she had to spread her kindness to others. A free car for a couple of days work was enough generosity for anyone.

Managing the companies and government agencies that tried to contact Everson was easy enough work for Dorothea — she was a master of bureaucracy and forging official letters — but the social aspect of his life was another matter entirely. He had adult children, whom he regularly corresponded with, and if their letters went unanswered, then there would be suspicion and, eventually, an investigation. Worse yet, Dorothea had no idea when Everson's last letters had gone out, so she didn't know how much of the true story his children already knew. The fantasy that she composed for them had to diverge from reality only after the point when the real Everson had died, to ensure that she didn't contradict anything he'd already written. So, in his letters, Everson now complained to his children of being sickly and bedridden; too ill to come and visit them but nowhere near to death's door, so they didn't have to rush to his side. In themselves, the letters may not have been enough to keep his children away, but with the supplementary material of Dorothea's new letters, introducing herself to the family and explaining how she was caring for Everson, they became convinced that he wasn't trying to spare their feelings. With this ongoing sickness, Everson wrote to them less frequently, but they still received regular updates on his health and outlook from the lovely woman that he'd settled down with. Dorothea calculated every letter written in Everson's handwriting to minimise her risk exposure, saving direct communications from beyond the grave for special occasions.

In the early months of 1986, Everson Gillmouth's body was discovered on the bank of the river by a fisherman, who quite rightly realised that the 6-foot long box looked almost exactly like a coffin. The police were summoned, but the body had already metamorphosed inside the chrysalis that Dorothea had created. With all of the moisture of the body trapped inside and more damp creeping in from the river, the California heat had putrefied the corpse in record time. The body couldn't be identified, and with no report of Everson even going missing, there was no way for them to make the connection. He was filed as a John Doe and buried in a pauper's grave, doomed to be forgotten. His only crime: trying to love a woman who was incapable of that emotion.

Back in Business

Despite all of the prohibitions against Dorothea operating a boarding house or caring for the elderly again, the needs of the state soon outweighed the rule of law. Social workers had already been quietly depositing homeless, addicted and otherwise hopeless cases on Dorothea from the moment that her doors reopened, and things only got busier once she had the whole operation up and running. The new boarding house was considerably smaller than the first, but the turnover was considerably higher, and given that Dorothea's main requirement from her tenants was for them to stay just long enough for her to redirect their benefits payments to her address, this worked out nicely for her designs. She was the last stop for people on the lowest rung of society, the last hint of a safety net before the homeless vanished entirely, never to return, and she used that position to prey on them. More than $5,000 was soon being deposited into her account each month in the form of dozens of different cheques, and she could easily have slipped back into high society if it weren't for the ongoing stigma attached to her name.

Dorothea began to schedule the absences of her residents. Alcoholics were the most common addicts in her care, and for the vast majority of them, recovery wasn't even a consideration. All of the mail to the house was intercepted by Dorothea before most of her guests had even woken from their stupor. She extracted any money or cheques from the post and handed out a stipend to her residents. It was through this money that she was able to control when they would next be arrested. All that she had to do to ensure that a drunk and disorderly charge stuck to one of her residents was to pay them out just enough so their latest binge would push them over the edge into belligerence.

She had the distance to the local bars and the drinking speed of her residents worked out. After she'd sent them off with cash in their pockets, it was a simple matter to call in an anonymous tip to the police about their behaviour, and like clockwork, they'd be picked up and would face 30 days of jail time — 30 days when Dorothea could rent out their room to somebody else while still collecting the jailed resident's benefit payments. She was careful not to have the same residents in constant trouble, but looking at it from the perspective of a criminal enterprise, it's quite obvious that she was running through a rotation based on how regularly each individual was up in front of a judge, but at the time, the government workers who were meant to be overseeing the care of her residents considered it to be a minor miracle that she kept them out of trouble for as long as she did.

Despite this constant turnover of bodies, Dorothea never managed to develop a bad reputation among the social workers that she encountered. They were well aware that she was taking on cases that nobody else wanted anything to do with, and if she lost some, or even most of them, then that was just inevitability doing its work. Some people were beyond saving — for the rest, there was Dorothea. She handed out homemade tamales to the homeless in the street outside her house and found little jobs for them to do in exchange for cash. She prepared lavish meals for her residents, and the few that stayed on with her described life in the house as being like a constant party. Alcohol and drugs were strictly prohibited, due to the nature of many of her residents' issues, but anything else was fair game, and the long days that would normally have worn an addict down were filled with chatter and games. Despite it never being her intention, Dorothea collected a loyal family of long-term residents who adored her and would do anything for her, up to and including lying to their own social workers to keep their place in her good graces. This was a problem. It wasn't that Dorothea didn't appreciate having a support network of people looking out for her interests, but she'd learned from her previous encounters with the law, and she now understood that those same people would gradually become aware of the patterns in her behaviour and the objectionable choices that she made. The longer they were in the house, the more that they would see, and the more that they saw, the more of a threat they became to Dorothea. Worse still, every client who lingered in her care was another room that she couldn't use for the never-ending parade of homeless addicts who were just passing through. She was enjoying her $5,000 a month income, but she wanted more. She'd always wanted more. She'd lost everything during her last arrest. All of her finery and her station in society had been stripped from her, and she was too old and too tired to move to some new town and start all over again. The world was becoming a smaller place by the 1980s, and the stories that she'd been able to leave at city limits earlier in her life would follow after her if she tried to flee now.

The ones who stayed trended a little older than her usual residents — they were getting too old for a life of constant motion, and in the comfort of Dorothea's home, they found the kind of retirement that they'd been longing for. Dorothy Miller and Benjamin Fink were the first to put roots down, settling into their respective rooms. Dorothy Miller was 64 years old, and she thought that she'd found a kindred spirit in Dorothea. The older woman was a Native American who'd developed a drinking problem early in life, one that plagued her through to these later days. She'd suffered heartbreak after heartbreak through the years, losing her young lover in a similarly tragic way to Dorothea's invented story. Despite being looked down on for her drinking problem, she was still a romantic at heart with endless poems committed to memory and ready to be recited at a moment's notice. Dorothea didn't know how to respond to the woman's interest in her life and found that her usual camouflage of tragedies just seemed to entice Dorothy further instead of putting her off. In Dorothy, Dorothea saw herself through a dark mirror, another version of herself with almost the same name, who'd actually been born into an ethnic minority, who'd actually suffered terrible loss in her life and who was still capable of such deep and profound emotion that just a few stanzas of a poem were enough to bring a tear to her eye. Her whole worldview was alien and dangerously antithetical to Dorothea's own, and she insisted on sharing as much time as possible with her landlady, sitting out on the porch smoking her hand-rolled cigarettes whenever Dorothea tried to escape her into the garden.

Importantly for Dorothea, the old woman suffered from night terrors as a result of her traumatic life and had been prescribed a not-inconsiderable dosage of sleeping pills to allow her to get some rest. It was with these pills that Dorothea carefully dosed Dorothy's cocktails up in her private apartment; the only place that alcohol was allowed in the building. It wasn't a particularly complex trap, but the bait was undeniably attractive. Offering an alcoholic a drink had to be the easiest scam she'd ever run.

As the resident who worked the hardest to be actively involved in Dorothea's life, this new 'sister' she'd acquired was the most likely to provide her with trouble further down the line, so it was almost inevitable that she was the first to draw the old woman's lethal attention, but it actually took Dorothea quite some time to successfully murder the woman. She'd built up considerable resistance to the cocktail of drugs that Dorothea was pouring down her throat over the years, so like the previous victims, she fell ill rather than dying outright. Of course, the sick fell into Dorothea's care within the house, allowing her to finish the job, but it still gave the other residents more time to become aware of the situation rather than Dorothy cleanly vanishing as intended.

At the age of 55, Benjamin wasn't drastically older than the usual transient residents, but he was more devoted to his own recovery from alcoholism than the majority. He would eat communal meals with the rest of the house but was otherwise quite solitary. He suffered from bouts of ill health after developing pneumonia while living on the streets — his lungs had never fully recovered from the damage, and he would often be forced to take to his bed for days at a time if he developed even so much as a sniffle. Dorothea would bring his meals to him in his room even though it was against her own rules for anyone to eat away from the group, and in that privacy, she was free to dose his food and force it down his throat as she saw fit. When his health worsened as a result of the drugging, Dorothea loudly announced to the home that she was taking him upstairs to take care of him, just as she had with Dorothy, but unlike Dorothy, the response was overwhelming apathy. Most of the transient residents didn't even know Ben because of his solitary nature, and it was rapidly approaching the point where none of them could recall Dorothy either. In much the same way as her previous victims, Dorothea killed Benjamin with a drug overdose.

The processing of each body replicated her preparation of Everson's corpse. They were sewn into the bedcovers, wrapped up in plastic sheeting and prepared for disposal within hours of their deaths, but then, they went no further. News did not travel so swiftly to Dorothea's ears as it used to. Her contacts within the police department had grown ever more distant since her return to civilian life, but even she had heard about the John Doe found at the side of the river out by the Garden Highway. If they had found Everson, they would find anyone else that she dumped like that, and eventually, evidence would point back to her. – All it would take was the identification of a single body to tie all the corpses to her guest house. She needed these bodies to disappear.

Of all the homeless population of Sacramento, the hulking alcoholic known only as 'Chief' was considered to be one of the most unwelcome. The one that shop owners would call the police to move along instead of trying to chase out themselves. The one who everyone knew had a criminal history. He existed at the crossroads between the homeless people that Dorothea loved to help and the ex-cons that she loved to exploit. Most importantly, to her, he loathed the police with a passion and would stonewall them whenever they encountered him. Others looked on Dorothea's adoption of the man as her personal handyman as a kind of madness — the natural end to her charity work stretched too far. They couldn't believe that a kind-hearted old woman could handle a hardened criminal like Chief; they fully expected to hear that he'd brutalised and robbed this beloved figure in the local community. Yet, as the days rolled by and nothing happened, the neighbours began to relax. The lumbering form of Chief became a regular addition to the usual workers in Dorothea's garden, and gradually, he became a part of the background noise, just like so many of the strange things that Dorothea did. With his physical strength, he became Dorothea's go-to assistant in all of her major remodelling of the garden. As they removed trees and shifted flowerbeds around, it was her mind directing Chief's huge hands. Sometimes she would have him working out there until late into the night, laying down the foul-smelling fertiliser that stank out the entire neighbourhood with the stench of rotting flesh until the soil had been turned over.

For all that Dorothea was a kindly soul, she had a territorial streak when it came to her garden. She wouldn't allow the neighbour's children onto her lawn and would cuss a streak if anyone stepped into her flowerbeds. Words that nobody would've expected a mild-mannered old landlady to bellow down from her porch to the street would redden people's ears.

Both Dorothy and Benjamin were buried in the back garden, under a flower bed. There was no way that Chief could've buried those bodies without knowing what they were, any more than there was any way that Dorothea could've been in any way unclear in her instructions to him about it. They were partners in crime from the moment that she let him know about those bodies. He was the muscle that she needed to dispose of the bodies, and she was the mastermind behind the whole operation, paying him a stipend out of the cheques that she collected each week to fund his drinking habit.

Time kept rolling on, and the money came rolling in. Troublesome tenants began vanishing at a much-increased rate unless they could be relied upon to find their way to jail with regularity, and Dorothea began trawling the local bars to look for new guests, just as she had in the early days. It got to the stage that she couldn't fill the rooms as fast as she was emptying them. The party atmosphere in the house began to turn colder as the place became increasingly empty and silent. Day after day, Chief came out of the house with more dirt dug up from the basement floor. Dorothea was replacing the dirt floor with concrete to keep the place cooler through the long summers, according to the story she spun for the neighbours. Yet, there seemed to be an awful lot more dirt than would be required to simply replace the surface of the basement floor. It was almost as though they were digging deep holes in the basement rather than just clearing the surface. It didn't really matter, of course. Once the concrete was poured, nobody would ever know for certain what had been done down there. With her routine now well established, Dorothea no longer had any reason to hold back from her murderous plotting. Chief could handle the clean-up; all that she needed were easy victims to keep the whole process flowing. For that, she turned her attention back to her old contacts in the care industry. If she could collect people who were already on the verge of death, as Benjamin had been, then it made her job as a murderer much easier, and as an added bonus, the people in extreme enough ill health to fall into the state-provided care system were always in receipt of the highest levels of benefits. On August 19, 1986, Betty Palmer was due for a regular check-up at the doctor, but she never showed up. She'd recently moved into the boarding house on F Street, but unlike the previous tenants who were accustomed to being treated like dirt, she'd come from a fairly stable background before mounting medical costs had robbed her of her home. When she discovered that Dorothea opened her mail and cashed her cheques, she immediately leapt into action, contacting the relevant department and ensuring that all future cheques required photographic identification to bank them. Betty hadn't gone so far as to report Dorothea to the police. She could understand why some of the other boarders required the kind of handling that Dorothea was trying to inflict on her, but she certainly hadn't lived 77 years handling her own finances just for some stranger to elbow her aside and take over now. The two of them had some terse words about the situation throughout the weeks, with Dorothea insisting that none of her residents would get special treatment, out of a desire for fairness. Dorothea had no idea how many people Betty was talking to about the situation — she had no control over where the woman went or who she went with. The whole scam in the boarding house only worked if Dorothea could maintain full control over all the moving pieces, and Betty was a wild card. Dorothea couldn't tell which way she would jump. It was unacceptable.

She invited Betty up to her parlour on the night of 18th August to have a few drinks and talk things through. Convinced that Dorothea wanted to bury the hatchet, Betty accepted the invitation — the last mistake she would ever make. Over the course of several hours, Dorothea plied her with cocktails full of sleeping pills and sweetened the medicine with all the sweet words that Betty wanted to hear, promising her the world and offering up all the apologies that the old woman wanted to hear. By the time that she was hustled down to her room to get changed and settled, Betty was feeling quite blissfully inebriated. With numb fingers, she fumbled out of her clothes and into her white nightgown. She collapsed before she could even reach her bed. When the room fell silent, Dorothea and her loyal henchman let themselves in with the master key and set to work.

The shoddy work of the previous corpses would be insufficient for Betty. It was quite possible that she would have people coming looking for her, people who already knew about the conflict with Dorothea and her landlady's motive to dispose of her. This body would have to be completely unidentifiable. Together, Dorothea and Chief set to work, spreading plastic sheeting across the floors and bringing out the handyman tools that the man had never touched before, despite his long tenure in that job. With saws and chisels, they cut through the old woman's neck in a sluice of arterial spray and removed her head. Next came the hands, and then the feet, along with a good portion of the lower legs. Any part of her body that might make for easy identification was removed and bagged up separately to be buried somewhere outside the city limits.

Only the unrecognisable mass of the old woman's torso remained, ready to join the other two victims in the garden now that the more convenient disposal option of the basement had been sealed off with concrete.

Chief roamed off with the smaller pieces on that same night, but it wouldn't be until the sunset on the 19th that they had an opportunity to move the main block of flesh into the garden. That was when they encountered the first real problem of the operation — the neighbours were out in their back gardens. The scorching Sacramento weather of that year had pushed everyone with a social life into more nocturnal patterns. Barbecues and clinking beer bottles were everywhere that Dorothea turned. The back garden had gone from the perfect refuge to Grand Central Station. There was no possibility of doing some late-night digging without it attracting all manner of unwanted attention. But, on the street at this time of night, there was practically nobody around — one car rolling by every hour, at most. Even if somebody was going about their night-time business, they were unlikely to say a thing about anything they saw, probably off conducting their own illicit affairs.

Working in tandem, Dorothea and Chief dug a shallow grave for the torso just a few feet away from the pavement in front of the house and covered it over just as quickly. If any passers-by saw them, then they never came forward to report the odd activities. To mark the grave of the troublesome woman and cover the freshly turned earth, Dorothea dragged a statue of St. Francis of Assisi into place.

For a few weeks, they lay low, actually conducting the business of the boarding house without any 'funny' activities, but when it became apparent that nobody had reported the old woman missing, Dorothea relaxed and went to cash her usual cheques, which was when she finally encountered the problem with Betty's payments. Without identification to prove that she was Betty, she could no longer deposit Betty's cheques. She played it off with a laugh about her faltering memory and came back the next day with exactly what she needed — Betty's ID, doctored to have Dorothea's picture in place of the dead woman's. With the added layer of security in place, the government didn't give a second thought to continuing to issue cheques to Betty even though they were out of touch, and Betty's near-constant doctor's appointments for the bad health that drove her to Dorothea's boarding house provided the perfect excuse whenever a social worker swung by to check on her welfare. Within a week, all of Betty's belongings were fenced, and the room was up for rent once more. Business rolled on as usual.

Partnerships Dissolved

If Chief had been a man of greater intelligence, then he may have realised that Dorothea did not keep the people that knew about her crimes around for very long. One by one, he'd helped her to bury everyone who might be able to implicate her in the murders. Everyone, except him. Perhaps he fell for the same deception as all of her other victims, that this little old woman was truly harmless. He knew that she could kill, but that didn't mean he believed she was capable of harming a strong man like him instead of the sickly and the elderly that she'd preyed on to date. It didn't even occur to him that anything might be untoward when she had him demolish a greenhouse in the back garden and prepare to lay a concrete slab over it.

In February of 1987, the house gained a new resident, who was unlikely to go anywhere soon — another one of the city's sickly who couldn't quite qualify for palliative care. Leona Carpenter was discharged from the hospital directly into Dorothea's care. At 77 years old, Leona had been fighting a long war with cancer, the last battle of which had been a prolonged brain surgery to remove the latest of her tumours. Dorothea stunned the ambulance drivers, who were dropping off to her, with the quality of care that she was prepared to offer. She'd set up one of the sofas in the living room as a daybed, and as they watched, she made a little nest of blankets for the old woman, who until that day had been a total stranger. Leona herself was completely overwhelmed by this kindness, singing Dorothea's praises to anyone who would listen.

Dorothea enjoyed this second-hand sympathy and praise for as long as it lasted, but after two weeks of waiting hand and foot on the old woman, she started to lose her patience. Leona didn't seem to be getting any better, and the few weeks of behaving like a nurse's aide again had reminded Dorothea why she'd quit that noble profession years before. She had no patience for the complaints and had a poor temperament for the constant demands. She delegated as many jobs as she could to the other residents, but even that wasn't enough to take the pressure off.

When it became apparent that nobody was going to come and check up on Leona so long as Dorothea continued to pass along good reports on her health, she sought the easiest way out of the situation. Leona was already dazed and confused from the operation, consuming more pills than the rest of the house combined on a daily basis anyway. It was hardly difficult for Dorothea to add a few more medications into the mix when her temper had frayed too far. She'd been prepared for this eventuality from the very beginning, with plastic sheeting placed underneath the blankets that she'd laid out for Leona's comfort. Another cocoon ready-made for the disposal of a corpse.

The new area destined to be covered in concrete wasn't prepared yet, so Dorothea and Chief dug a shallow hole between a tree and the garden's border fence, fully intending to relocate the remains to a more permanent resting place later when they had more time. Leona's fragile and sickness-withered body dropped into it without a trace.

Carol Durning was the next resident to receive Dorothea's attention. She'd arrived in the boarding house at the start of the year and had done her best to keep her head down, but the fact that she was still there after three months seemed to concern Dorothea. Carol seemed entirely immune to Dorothea's dubious charms — she'd been through enough in her life to ignore any social pressure from the old woman or from the other residents to conform, and she was out of her room like a shot every time that the mailman came around. Because of all this, Dorothea was careful around Carol, taking care to keep any information about her illegal activities well away from her since she couldn't be trusted. Keeping her isolated throughout her tenure in the boarding house should've dealt with the problem, but if anything, it just made matters worse. Instead of being driven out as a pariah, Carol became a rallying point for those who didn't like Dorothea's regime. Even residents who'd gone with the flow for years began questioning the rightness of Dorothea controlling their state-given money.

As a new arrival, James Gallop, fresh out of the hospital, was one of the residents who rallied to her. He argued back and forth with Dorothea about his money, demanding that she turn it over to him, else he'd report her to the police. Dorothea couldn't afford to have policemen wandering around her house, not anymore. She no longer had the clout at City Hall or the commissioner's office to make her problems disappear. Where before she'd only had figurative skeletons in her closet, she now had literal decomposing corpses in her garden. James would have to be dealt with. Like most of Dorothea's preferred victims, he was in ill health. He'd survived cancer and a massive heart attack in the year before he was passed into her care, and the boarding house was the first place outside of a hospital that he could've called home for many years before that. His health problems had destroyed any trace of a life that he'd had before, friends and family falling out of touch as he lingered on the verge of death day after day, week after week, month after month. At 62 years old, he was entirely alone, and by the time that he arrived in Dorothea's care, all trace of the man he was before, everything that he had been, was seared away by his burning primal need for survival. He wasn't suspicious of Dorothea's attempts at kindness — he'd been on the receiving end of that cold sympathy from medical staff for so long, it felt like his normal state of interaction by this point, but he was fiercely protective of his independence now that he was starting to get it back. He took his medicine by himself. He wanted control of his own money, and he kept his room in the boarding house as a private space that Dorothea was clearly not welcome in. It made it very difficult to kill him. She managed to slip some sleeping pills to him in lieu of painkillers, but he quickly became wise to that and was heard loudly complaining that her medicine always made him sleepy. He complained long and loud enough that Dorothea didn't dare to make another failed attempt at his life. She had to wait to make certain that the next time, she would be successful.

Dorothea was so fixated on dealing with the immediate threat of James that the greater threat of Carol completely slipped her mind. Carol had slipped through her fingers. After six months of being treated like garbage, Carol moved out of the boarding house of her own accord, though Dorothea would later claim to have evicted her. She'd seen very little of what happened in the house on F Street, and she remained tight-lipped about what she had seen. Even so, she was still a witness who'd slipped out of Dorothea's reach, which sent Dorothea into a spiral of panic.

Almost immediately after Carol's departure in July, Dorothea ground up a lethal dose of sleeping pills and mixed them into James's food. It was a risky move to poison someone in full view of the whole house, and if he'd noticed and complained then she might very well have been exposed, but with the depleted number of guests in the house, Dorothea decided to take that risk, regardless of the consequences.

Using Dorothy and Ruth's identification cards, modified with her picture, in addition to her contacts in the medical profession, Dorothea had been able to secure multiple sources of sleeping pills. She stockpiled many different types of medication under the guise of needing them to care for her residents and the community members who still sought out La Doctora for their care rather than trusting the American medical establishment. This meant that when she committed to killing James, she was more than capable of delivering a dose that could've killed him, right there at the table. As it was, he didn't pass out until after dinner, when the group had moved through to the living room to listen to music. He may have been dead there and then, or Dorothea may have plied him with more drugs once she had dragged him off to her rooms. Either way, Chief was back the next morning, patting down a fresh patch of turned soil in the back garden before the sun had even risen.

Throughout this whole campaign of murder, the complaints about the odious smells in Dorothea's boarding house had continued to be voiced. She'd blamed her fertilisers, dead rats under the floorboards and trouble with the drains to various neighbours, at different times — the story ever-shifting as she spat out excuses far too casually, assuming that the neighbours never spoke amongst themselves, assuming that she was the centre of the world around which all other people orbited. She'd spent a lifetime rewriting her history as she saw fit, remaking the world to suit the story that she was trying to tell. It was hardly surprising that she no longer saw other people as human, only as backing characters in her own grand drama. After all, a few years down the line when she told a story about them, they could be completely changed by just a twist of the tongue. Only Dorothea's fantasy world was real to her; everything else was just a nuisance to be navigated.

With the plot out back finally ready for the concrete to be laid down, Dorothea decided to close another chapter of the story that would never be told. After another hard day of work out in the back garden, Dorothea invited Chief up to her room for some drinks. By this point in their relationship, this was a fairly regular occurrence, certainly not something that would raise the eyebrows of any of the residents, nor of Chief himself. Dorothea kept a stock of good liquor in her private bar up in her rooms, kept under lock and key throughout the day to keep any sticky-fingered alcoholics from creeping up the stairs. It was a selection that Chief was always excited to sample. Dorothea made up fancy cocktails so potent they could make the hair on the back of his neck stand up, things that made the rot-gut whiskey that he drank every other night pale in comparison.

They settled into their usual routine of drinks and companionable silence a little later than usual since Chief had worked through until dusk to get everything ready for tomorrow's concrete pouring. The alcohol did its soothing work, loosening up all the tight muscles across his back, and Dorothea seemed even more pleasant than usual, refilling his glass over and over without his having to make the usual hints to get things flowing. If he'd been a smarter man, he might've realised that she was being uncharacteristically accommodating, but as it was, he just felt like he was being rewarded for a job well done. There were a lot of bodies out there in the back garden, under the place where the greenhouse used to be — more bodies than he could even remember burying, in truth — and Dorothea was probably relieved that she could finally put them all behind her. He'd never bought her story about burying the bodies as a benefits scam. He knew that she had to be killing the people that lived here because there were just too many bodies getting planted out in the garden and the basement to have died of natural causes. Just because he knew, it didn't mean he had to speak about it. The one thing his time in the army had taught him was that you didn't open your mouth about things that didn't directly concern you; not if you didn't want trouble raining down on you from unexpected directions and sniper shots bouncing off trees beside your head that couldn't possibly have come from the enemy camp.

He didn't usually drift into self-reflection and painful memories when he drank — that was half the reason that he drank — but for some reason, that night, he found himself drifting off into a flowing river of them. He was so lost in thought that he barely even flinched when he felt Dorothea touch him. His whole world felt like it was wrapped up in cotton wool — nothing was quite real; nothing could hurt him anymore. He didn't even realise that he'd been walked through to the bedroom, didn't even think that the plastic sheeting laid over the blankets was anything out of the ordinary. This was how he'd always seen Dorothea's bed. Every time he'd been in here to drag out a body, the plastic had been there. He was drugged so heavily that alarm bells didn't even start to ring when she laid him down and started wrapping him up. He could feel his breath, trapped wet between his face and the plastic sheeting. He couldn't move his arms or his legs, but he wasn't sure if that was because the wrap was holding them in place or that he was too disconnected from his own body to get his limbs to obey him. Only when Dorothea wrapped the sheets and blankets around him and began to stitch did fear finally rear up inside him. Only when the light of the bulb swaying overhead was blotted out by cloth and the looming shadow of the old woman did even a hint of awareness creep through. She was killing him. Perhaps he was already unconscious, and this was just a dream. For all that he knew, he was already buried out in the garden, and the hot, laborious breaths that he was trying to draw inside the plastic were the last of his air.

The next morning, Dorothea went out alone to pour the concrete and seal off the fresh-turned soil that had once been the garden shed. She had plans to put a new shed up on top of it eventually, but there was no rush for that. It would take her some time to select a new handyman for the property, one who'd be up for doing that kind of heavy work. It was such a shame that Chief had just vanished in the night without a word to anyone. She expressed her disappointment to anyone who would listen when they asked after the hulking man who'd become a fixture of the neighbourhood. She'd given him his pay for the week, and he'd run off without so much as a thank you, and nobody had seen him again. Compared to the expansive nature of Dorothea's usual tall tales, it was a bit of an anti-climax. It was such a bland story that it soon faded from everyone's collective memory. They'd expected Chief's presence to end with a bang, with a robbery or a murder. Instead, he'd faded away without a sound, just another homeless man drifting on when he grew tired of the place where he'd settled.

The relationship had been of great benefit to Dorothea over the last few years, but now she was becoming paranoid, and the greed that had always driven her actions had kicked into overdrive. She didn't want to share the takings from her ingenious criminal enterprise with some lowlife who couldn't understand the complexities of forging a cheque, and she couldn't afford to have anyone who understood the full picture except her, walking around. Even now at the height of her hubris, when she felt at her most invulnerable, she was planning her defence should one of the bodies ever be discovered, and that entire plan hinged on her version of events being the only one that was ever told.

She took one night of rest after spending a whole day out in the back of the house spreading concrete within the wooden frame Chief had set up. She then went back to trawling the bars for new customers. Her expensive tastes couldn't be satisfied without a never-ending flow of new boarders. The small comforts that had made her feel more secure after her chaotic childhood had become more and more important as the years went by, and she'd lost the respect of the people she'd tried so hard to curry favour with. They consumed her, and in turn, the lives of one resident after another.

Without Chief on call, the disposal of bodies became a pressing concern for Dorothea once more. The rate of her murders went from a tide to a trickle, overnight. But, they certainly didn't stop. Dorothea would never stop now that she had a taste of how easy murder could make her life. Like the joiner who only has a hammer and views all problems as a nail, Dorothea looked upon her extensive medicine cabinet as a cure-all, not only for physical ailments but also for any troubles in her life. Through killing, she could control absolutely everything. She could make the chaos of the world into order. She could make it all fit into her story perfectly.

In October of 1987, Vera Martin arrived in the boarding house, signed all of the paperwork that Dorothea presented to her and was never seen in public again. Before now, there'd always been a window of opportunity for escape, a chance for the new arrivals to meet and greet the other residents of the boarding house and get settled in before they mysteriously moved along. Vera never even got the chance to sit down to one of Dorothea's famous home-cooked meals. Guided directly upstairs, once her belongings were locked away in one of the many empty rooms, she was nestled in Dorothea's living room with a cocktail in her hand before she could even be noticed. She was drugged, bedded and wrapped so swiftly that Dorothea forgot to search her for valuables before dragging her down the stairs to be stowed away.

Homer Myers was another of Dorothea's long-time residents, but he managed to miss her lethal attentions by virtue of staying quiet and mostly obedient during his two-year tenure at the boarding house. When she handed him the forms that were required for her to cash his social security cheques, he didn't argue with her, he just misplaced them. When she tried again a few months later, he misplaced them all over again. Eventually, she stopped trying, judging the man to be too slow-witted to present a threat to her — an assumption that may not have been entirely unfair, given that after her disposal of Chief, she convinced Homer to dig a grave in her garden without him ever realising its purpose, even when no peach tree was ever planted in the 6-foot-deep hole he'd dug in one sweltering afternoon.

When Dorothea hauled the corpse out and began shovelling dirt down onto her, the watch on Vera's wrist was still ticking. Beneath the soil, in the dark, it would go on ticking, counting off the moments until it saw the light of day once more. It wouldn't be long. Even preying on the most vulnerable in society, Dorothea's murderous ways would not go unnoticed forever. All it would take was one victim who was not so easily forgotten.

Mama's Boy

Alvaro 'Bert' Montoya was a quiet man, speaking almost exclusively in his native Spanish and mostly to himself. He was developmentally disabled and schizophrenic, with a child-like intelligence that meant most of the conversations he did manage to carry were with people nobody else could see. Even in his fiercest arguments with the voices in his head, Alvaro was gentle, talking calmly and politely, regardless of what they were urging him to do. His mother, back in Puerto Rico, had instilled a solid sense of manners in him before letting him slip out into the world. She must've known that, if he ever appeared to be anything other than a gentle giant, people would turn on him in an instant. With wild, white hair and an overgrown beard, Alvaro struck a frightening figure as he slurred and staggered his way down the Sacramento streets, communicating with others almost exclusively in animalistic grunts and moans. The whole world saw Alvaro as another of the hopeless alcoholics who littered the streets of Sacramento, but the truth was he'd never even tasted alcohol.

His deceptive appearance led to him being passed from pillar to post by the social security system with no success. He spent his nights sleeping in a large shed, which was provided by the Volunteers of America, on Front Street and was surrounded on all sides by dangerous alcoholics and drug addicts. One of those alcoholics took a liking to Alvaro, despite his general inability to communicate, and managed to coax a few words in broken English out of him. He believed that Alvaro had introduced himself as Alberto, so immediately took to calling him 'Bert' — a name that stuck with him from that point onwards. While they could do nothing to help Bert due to his lack of addictions, he still spent long periods during the day lingering around the local detox centre, where he was given a hot meal and a little guidance by the kindly staff. It wasn't much of a life, and the chaos of it all seemed to be exacerbating his symptoms. He grew less and less verbal with every passing day, turning ever inward and speaking only to the voices screaming inside his head.

One member of the Volunteers of America took a shining to Bert, recognising that he was a kindly soul suffering from a terrible affliction. Judy Moise had spent much of her adult life helping the homeless and destitute of Sacramento navigate the intricacies of the system that was meant to protect them. In cases like Bert's, when the person she was trying to help might have had direct exposure to that system, things became even more complicated. If Bert had come into the USA illegally, then there was a risk that any official enquiries that Judy made might lead to him being deported and losing the already minimal support network that he had in place. Every step that she took forward, she had to take two back to keep Bert out of the eyes of the government. She harvested information from Bert in short barks when she was able to corner him in the Front Street shed. Between his broken English and her high school Spanish, communication went slowly, but one day at a time, tiny snippets of information gradually added up to a full picture. Bert was from Puerto Rico. He was born there in September of 1936. His full name was Alvaro José Rafael González Montoya. Most importantly, from Judy's perspective, some calls to the American Embassy in San Jose, Costa Rica, had revealed that his mother had legally immigrated to the USA with her son and daughter in 1962. He was a legal citizen of America, which meant that he was entitled to all of the care and support that any native-born citizen would've been. She was able to furnish him with photographic identification and all of the information he needed to apply for social security cheques and medical support. It wasn't much, but it was the first step towards a better future for Bert. For the first time since she'd met him, Judy had hope that his life might get better.

The next challenge was to find permanent housing for Bert where he would receive the level of care that he required, somewhere that his eccentricities wouldn't see him ostracised by those around him. It was then that she came across the name of Dorothea Puente for the first time. Her boarding house on F Street had a bad reputation further up the echelons of the social work department, where news of her criminal convictions had spread, but down on the street, nobody cared about the political posturing. All that they were interested in was helping their clients, and from the description that Judy had received, Dorothea was everything that she needed. Still, she wouldn't trust her beloved Bert to just anyone. She visited the boarding house to see the lay of the land for herself.

She was stunned by what she found. The old Victorian house, painted in pastel colours, looked little different from all the others around it, but on the inside, everything changed. There was music playing, and Dorothea was handing out home-made tamales to her guests as they laughed and played a game of cards together. It was everything that the care system promised to be but had never quite managed to fulfil. It was like a dream come true for Judy — the perfect place for Bert. She secured some time alone with Dorothea in her strictly regimented kitchen, gratefully received a cup of fresh-made coffee and explained Bert's situation in detail.

The surprises kept on coming. There was a tear in the corner of Dorothea's eye by the time that the story had been told, and she was already nodding. 'I will take care of this poor boy. I remember what it was like to immigrate to this country and to be left all alone like him. My mother died when I was young, too. Always too young. I know just how to take care of men with these troubles. I have had so many through here before. He will get everything that he needs. I will take such good care of him, I promise you'.

Two days later, Bert moved in. Judy couldn't believe how quickly things were moving and was even more surprised when she realised that Dorothea was paying for Bert out of her own pocket until his social security cheques started coming through. The next time that Judy visited, he was in a full set of new clothes, his hair was washed and combed, and even his wild beard had been tamed. Whatever Dorothea was doing was working. He received three square meals a day, and even the other residents who'd sung Dorothea's praises the first time that Judy came through couldn't help but wax lyrical about the special treatment that Bert received. The kitchen was usually Dorothea's sacred space, where mere mortals were not allowed to enter, but every day, she had Bert in there helping her.

His days were filled with gentle garden work, simple tasks around the building and good company. Dorothea was always by his side, chatting away to him in Spanish or English as he switched back and forth involuntarily, answering every one of his outbursts, no matter how irrational, with her calm and measured voice. The two of them seemed to radiate peace, and for a moment, Judy felt like fate had brought the two of them together — the woman who needed someone to care for, whom would love her unconditionally in return, and the simple man terrified of the world outside. She couldn't believe how lucky the choice to place him here had been. Unbelievably, Bert was able to talk to Judy clearly for the first time, stringing together whole sentences and showing that he understood not only where he was but also who he was and what had happened to him. There was talk of taking him to a doctor to get him started back up on an anti-psychotic medication now that he was capable of taking care of himself again. At that, he proudly showed Judy his fingernails — they were clean, and he had cut them himself for the first time in years.

When Dorothea left the house, she would often take Bert along with her to carry her bags or just to keep her company. He became a constant presence in her life, the kind of man whom she'd hoped that Chief might have become if it hadn't been for his unfortunate selfish streak. In return, Dorothea genuinely seemed to care for him. The other houseguests had often seen her feeding stray cats in the neighbourhood. In Bert, it seemed that she'd found a stray to adopt who might actually return her efforts and affections. It all would've seemed quite sweet if it hadn't been for the places that Dorothea was taking him.

In March of 1988, Dorothea and Bert walked downtown to the Social Security Administration building, where Dorothea listed herself as Alvaro's cousin on his paperwork and arranged for all of his money to be deposited into her account. A quick stop off at social security department's mandated psychiatrist, to prove that Bert was not mentally capable of managing his own finances, and the deal was done.

Social workers came by to check in on Bert shortly after this change was made, not out of any suspicion but simply because it was on their schedule to do so. They were amazed by the improvements that had been made, both in terms of his behaviour and his appearance. They began discussing the possibility of getting Bert back onto the medication that would allow him to completely control the symptoms of his schizophrenia, but after all of his time in the Detox centre, Bert had absorbed a few of the lessons that were being bandied about. Drugs were bad. He didn't want drugs. They would make him sick. They would hurt him. He was scared of needles. He choked when he tried to swallow pills. He didn't like the taste of them. Arguing with him about it was as hopeless as trying to dispute the facts with a stubborn child. His opinion couldn't be changed.

The social workers were in an awkward situation with Dorothea. They knew that, legally, the situation in the boarding house was a little precarious, but the service that Dorothea was offering to the local community drastically outweighed the need for any punitive enforcement of the law in their eyes. Whatever Dorothea had done clearly wasn't that bad, since the parole officer who visited regularly had no issues with her managing the care and finances of all these people. They assumed that the system was working as intended, so they ignored the little rule violations, for the greater good.

For the parole officers, who heard all about the comings and goings of the social work department, the same thing was happening. They assumed that nobody would be lodging clients with Dorothea if she weren't behaving in an upstanding manner, so she was given a free pass on the blatant parole violations of running a boarding house, caring for the elderly and sickly and handling social security cheques — the only restrictions that'd actually been placed on the woman when she was set free. With her white hair, missing teeth and grandmotherly demeanour, it was hard to look at Dorothea and picture her as a criminal of any sort. She slipped through the cracks of both the parole and social care systems, manipulating the individuals that she met into believing, above all else, that she was harmless and keeping any hint of impropriety unreported so that when concerns did rear their ugly heads, there would be no corroborating evidence.

When she went in for a facelift, she took Bert along to carry her bags and sleep in the chair by her hospital bed, even though he was quite terrified of hospitals. She didn't want to leave him alone, even for the one night that she was going to be away. Just as she had cared for him when he first arrived in the house, so did he care for her through her convalescence, fetching and carrying whatever she required and having free run of the whole house, even acting as her hands in the dinner preparations that she watched over with her peering eyes surrounded by bandages. She recovered from the operation in record time and switched her matronly wardrobe for something a little more stylish and glamorous — the kind of clothes that she'd wished she could afford back in her 20's and 30's, things that she could afford now that she had so many social security cheques feeding into her account. Perfumes and the latest fashion from Paris filled her upstairs room. She was taking very good care of herself.

With his hospital ordeal over, Bert was glad to return to his old task of tending to the garden, digging a deep hole for a new tree that Dorothea planned to plant in one corner to create a shady overlook, the same peach tree that was meant to be planted weeks before when Vera was consigned to the earth. This time, the hole was broader and meant to hold a larger mass, wide enough that Bert could stand right inside it and spin around without any trouble. That was the specific size that she'd instructed him to dig it. She showered Bert with praise after all of his hard work, indulging him with the treats and sweets that he loved so much and helping him to wash himself up afterwards. It didn't surprise anyone in the boarding house when Bert was invited up to her parlour after dinner in the evenings. It was obvious that she had a great affection for the man, even if he wasn't entirely capable of returning that affection in kind. He was never up in her rooms until late because her sense of propriety wouldn't allow it — even if the man in her chambers happened to have the mental capacity of a small child — but he came down the stairs smiling every night that she invited him up to visit, and her records could be heard warbling through the house every single evening they were together. Some of the other residents joked that she was teaching him how to dance.

With the big hole already dug for the new tree, Bert's work in the garden became less frequent and more sporadic. He would work through a morning then have to go for a lie down in the shade for a few hours to recover. Even though he was in the best physical health that he'd been in for years, he seemed to be drained of his energy. To the visitors meant to watch for his welfare, it seemed that he was just becoming more and more subdued as his psychosis lost its hold on him, and he was certainly getting much calmer and more capable of conversing without his usual twitching and fidgeting as a result of whatever changes Dorothea had made. The only one who seemed to be genuinely concerned was Bert, and he lacked the skills to communicate that concern to anyone who might help. With less work to do in the garden, and Dorothea's interest in him seeming to wane as she emotionally distanced herself from him, Bert found that he had free time to himself again. He began to roam the streets as he used to but with a calm home to return to. All of the bellowing and braying voices that had once sounded down every alley, driving him ever off course, had faded to silence. He was able to stroll from destination to destination without faltering. He soon became a regular visitor to the detox centre again, where he enjoyed catching up with all of his old friends now that he was more capable of upholding his side of the conversation. They, too, were amazed at the changes that had come over Bert, amazed and delighted.

One of the workers who'd taken a personal interest in Bert was surprised to find that the man spoke English with some proficiency and could follow almost the whole conversation that they shared, asking for clarification only a few times. It was this nurse that Bert tried to confide in about his dwindling strength and stamina, talking about being tired all the time now that Dorothea had him working in the garden. He made the wrong causal link, so the nurse couldn't help him. Of course he was tired after working in the garden all day — from anyone else, the complaint would've seemed like a non-statement — but still, the nurse tried to draw more information out of Bert. Eventually, there was an abrupt change of track.

Bert complained that Mama was giving him medicine that he didn't like. That set alarm bells ringing in the nurse's mind, so he kept Bert from going back home to Dorothea. Instead, he called the boarding house and asked her to come down and collect Bert so that they could have a chat about his progress. When Dorothea arrived, expecting to be applauded once more for all of the changes that she'd made in Bert's life, she was instead ambushed by the nurse, demanding to know what she was dosing the poor man with.

The sweet grandmother vanished in an instant as Dorothea's temper flared. 'You want him? You want him back here? You want to tell me how to run my house? How to run my business? You can have him! He is so much trouble, all day I'm watching him. You take him. He can come stay here, and you see how well he does.' She even turned on her beloved Bert. 'You want to stay here? You want to complain about how I take care of you? That's fine. You stay here with all these people. See how well they take care of you. See how well you sleep on the floor here instead of your bed back home.'

The nurse drew Bert out of the office so they could talk through his options. From the hallway, he could see the rows of cots set up for addicts and alcoholics — the same people who'd brutalised Bert into non-verbal communication, the kind of life that he wouldn't wish on anyone. 'You should say sorry and go home with Miss Dorothea. She takes good care of you, doesn't she?'

Bert nodded with a mournful expression on his face. He may not have liked the medicine, but he couldn't deny that Mama took good care of him when she wasn't forcing him to take the pills.

The two of them left the detox centre holding hands. Dorothea still glowering at the staff, but her scowl softening when she turned to her precious Bert. They strolled off down the road towards home, and that was the last time that anyone saw him alive.

On their return to the boarding house, Dorothea took him directly up to her room and began force-feeding him sleeping pills. Bert didn't want to take them, but the nurse, his only other guiding light, had told him that he should, that he should obey Mama no matter what she told him to do. Before long, he was feeling sleepy, so Mama said that he could come and have a lie down in her bed until he felt better. He was surprised. Mama never let him into her bedroom, and he tried to fumble his way through an excuse, but his mouth no longer seemed to be obeying him, and the voices in his head that could usually be relied on to warn him if there was any trouble had fallen completely silent. He was alone in an echoing quiet, but he wasn't afraid because his Mama was right there holding his hand. She was right there as he lay down on the bed, and she was right there as she bundled him up in sheets and blankets to keep him warm. Even when the plastic sheeting was wrapped around the outside of the little tortilla she'd made out of him, he didn't stir, and he didn't startle. He had nothing to be afraid of. Mama would always take care of him.

The next morning, the long-awaited peach tree arrived. It was planted in the hole that Bert had dug, a hole that had become considerably shallower overnight, and several of the residents helped Dorothea to bed it down with the heap of soil that she'd prepared. Some of them were surprised that Bert wasn't among their number since he was a long-time favourite garden helper of Dorothea's. When they asked, Dorothea began to cry. He had left. Her baby boy had run away in the night. He'd been contacted by his sister and her husband, and they wanted to take over his care. The whole house rallied around her in sympathy. Everyone knew that she had a very special relationship with Bert, even if they couldn't quite grasp why.

Even if nobody else had that same connection with the man, his presence was sorely missed within the house. If nothing else, he was a soothing influence on Dorothea's excesses. Without his mournful eyes on her, there was nothing to stop her from withdrawing from her acquired family entirely, sinking back into her fantasies of glitz and glamour. He'd been her anchor to the real world, a solid physical presence so that she couldn't live entirely in her memories, both real and invented. Without Bert to keep her in the present, all of her worst selfish habits could come to the fore.

Dearly Missed

In October of 1988, just a few days after Bert's disappearance, Judy showed up at the house unannounced, looking for him. Her emotional connection to the man hadn't diminished just because Dorothea had forged such a close relationship with Bert, and she liked to stop in from time to time, just to see how he was doing. She was dismayed to find that Bert was nowhere to be seen. The other residents shied away from answering any questions, most of them heading off to their rooms when Judy arrived, and it was only when Dorothea finally emerged from the sanctuary of her kitchen that Judy got an explanation. Bert had taken ill, and he was laid up in his bed and sleeping right now. It was nothing serious, nothing to worry about, and Dorothea promised that she was taking the very best care of her boy. Something about the delivery of that lie sounded off to Judy, whether it was the lack of sorrow in Dorothea's voice or the attempts to garner second-hand sympathy and praise by listing off all the things that she was doing for Bert. Judy made a note to herself to check up on Bert as soon as possible.

When her schedule over the following days prevented this, Judy got in touch with Peggy Nickerson, Bert's social worker, and asked her to investigate the situation. At first, Peggy got the same story as Judy when she phoned asking to speak to Bert, but as the days rolled on and she still couldn't speak to him, she became increasingly concerned about this illness that had taken hold of him and asked Dorothea if he might not be better off in a hospital. The fury and ultimatums that had driven off interference from the detox centre workers wouldn't work against an official from the social work department. Dorothea had to think fast — never her strong suit — and the lie that she'd concocted was as simple as it was stupid. Bert was actually feeling much better, and he'd left town.

Judy was at Dorothea's door the next day, demanding information. Overnight, Dorothea had concocted a whole new story, and now, with Judy as a waiting audience, she began to spin her webs of deceit. After his bout of illness, Bert had been quiet and introspective, regretting his past and longing to mend broken bridges. He'd called up his sister, and the very same day, she and her husband had shown up and taken him away to Mexico with them to visit the rest of his family. With any other volunteer and any other transient, the story might've landed, but Judy knew Bert's story inside and out. She knew he'd never been to Mexico in his life, had no family there and definitely didn't know his sister's phone number. She had spent months trying to track down Bert's sister and had come to believe that the woman was living somewhere outside of the USA. She left without questioning Dorothea's story, but she was certain that the old woman was lying, even if she couldn't work out why.

After Judy shared this latest information with Peggy, the social worker began to make regular calls to Dorothea for an update on Bert's location. The family holiday could only stretch for so many weeks before he would have to come home, so she needed a new story, and this one would require more depth. The next time that Peggy rang, in early November, Dorothea informed her with faux delight that Bert had decided he wanted to stay with his sister and her husband from now on. They would live together at their house in Utah, and Bert would no longer require any of them to watch over him because he had his beloved family back in his life. Peggy judged this to be implausible and demanded contact details from Dorothea so that the story could be corroborated by Bert's family. Backed into a corner, Dorothea claimed that she couldn't just go around giving out phone numbers to strangers and abruptly terminated the call.

If Peggy wasn't suspicious before, now she was certain that something strange was going on in Dorothea's boarding house. She contacted Judy and asked her to start making some enquiries about Dorothea to see what the people on the street knew about her, trying to gauge exactly what kind of trouble poor Bert might have gotten himself into. But, before that investigation could get any further, Peggy received a call in her office that should've set her mind at ease.

Dorothea had always had a network of ready bodies to call on in the lowest caste of society. Every transient, ex-cons and addict knew her name, and that she was good for a few bucks here and there if you were willing to put in some work. Donald Anthony was just one of the many men that she'd hired to do odd jobs through the years, and while he'd never lived under her roof, the halfway house that he spent his nights in was just a few streets away. He was a convenient voice for her to put on the phone. Unfortunately for Dorothea, you get what you pay for when it comes to voice actors, and while Donald successfully delivered the news that Bert was going to be staying with him and his wife — Bert's sister — he used the name 'Bert' repeatedly on the call, even though his family would've had no reason to call him that. When he was signing off, he actually said his own name instead of the false one that Dorothea had provided to him. This call was the straw that broke the camel's back; Dorothea's behaviour had gone from odd to outright suspicious. It took only a few minutes of calling around for Peggy to learn the identity of her prank caller and his connection to Dorothea, and it took her even less time to decide what she had to do next. She called the police.

It was entirely luck that the call was patched through to Detective John Cabrera, the only man in the Sacramento Police Department who'd ever led the hunt for a serial killer before, hunting Morris Solomon less than a year before and uncovering the pattern of murders that would convict that handyman of the murder of six women across the city. It seemed to Cabrera that this was probably just a case of confusion rather than anything more sinister. Still, he went out to do his due diligence, arranging to visit the boarding house that day to interview Dorothea and her guests and get to the bottom of the missing person's case where the person had already been repeatedly accounted for.

At the house, Dorothea had all of her guests out on display, laughing, smoking and playing games in the communal areas. Snacks were being circulated, and the landlady seemed to have returned to her former friendly disposition. For the few long-term guests, this was a wonderful return to form, and they wouldn't even consider looking the gift horse in the mouth. For the newer guests, it was a new treat to be handled with such kindness by Dorothea, whom they knew had been in a bit of a slump ever since Bert had left. It all seemed very pleasant, but Cabrera knew the dark secrets that could hide under a well-maintained exterior. He took each of the guests to a separate room and interviewed them. Even in the privacy of their own rooms, none of the guests deviated from the story that Dorothea had provided, although a few of them did cast nervous glances towards the door, half expecting somebody to come bursting in if they said the wrong thing. In itself, it wasn't enough for Cabrera to cause any more trouble, but it did make him discount the idea that nothing untoward was happening in the house.

One of the last residents to be interviewed was John Sharp, an alcoholic who'd been under Dorothea's care for the longest of any of them. In his interview with Cabrera, he toed the party line carefully, reciting the story of Bert's journey to Mexico and then Utah, verbatim, and praising Dorothea loudly enough that it made the detective wonder if the old woman had her ear pressed to the door. When it became obvious that he wasn't going to get anything useful from Sharp, Cabrera was ready to leave empty-handed, but before he could step out into the hallway, the man reached over and shook that empty hand, slipping a tiny handwritten note into the officer's palm. Cabrera pocketed it quickly before saying his goodbyes to Dorothea, who was all smiles knowing that her deception had gone off without a hitch this time.

Out in his car, parked up the street, Cabrera finally opened up the little note that Sharp had passed him. It was succinct. 'She is making us lie for her'.

Later in the day, when Sharp made his regular trip to the store for cigarettes, Cabrera pulled up and offered him a lift. That soon turned into a stop at a cafe so the two of them could have a little chat. In the intervening hours, Cabrera had looked into Sharp's history and confirmed that the man had no particular grudge against Dorothea that he might now be trying to air — it seemed that the man was legitimate.

His story was fragmented and unclear at first — just little snippets of odd events that only took on sinister undertones when the whole picture emerged. Stories about holes being dug in the gardens and filled in again overnight, about the concrete poured out without any real reason to be laying concrete, one or two instances where guests took sick and then moved up the stairs into Dorothea's rooms before vanishing in the night just as surely as the holes in the gardens did, all underlain with the sickly sweet scent of rot, blamed on the drains, on the rats, on the fish emulsion on the lawn. A dozen little excuses why the people couldn't be reached. A dozen petty complaints about letters being opened if they looked like they might contain a cheque. Dorothea's extravagant spending. Her perfumes and top-shelf liquor. A tapestry of individual threads that meant nothing but that could be wound together to create a very suspicious-looking picture.

It was enough to launch a more thorough investigation into Dorothea, one that soon turned up the full breadth of her criminal history stretching all the way back to her original prostitution charges. That was all ancient history as far as Cabrera was concerned, but the more recent charges, the drugging and robbery, the forgery and the fraud, those all pointed to a more dangerous situation in the boarding house. He contacted Dorothea's parole officer and discovered the legal prohibitions against her maintaining the boarding house. More threads were woven into the tapestry, and the picture looked more and more sinister with every passing minute.

Collecting the parole officer and a few good men in uniform, Cabrera headed back to the house on F Street with shovels in the backseat. It was 11th November 1988. He didn't have enough for a warrant, not yet. He might be able to force the closure of the boarding house if it came to it, but he was hoping that it wouldn't be necessary given how charming Dorothea was and how content the other residents seemed to be. If he could search the house and find nothing else that enflamed his suspicion, then he might be able to walk away and let everyone get on with their lives in peace. That was a big 'if'.

When they arrived at Dorothea's boarding house, she welcomed them all in and offered them coffee. If there was anything that she could do to help them give comfort to the people who were worried about her precious Bert, she'd be delighted to help in any way that she could. She led them to his room, as yet unlet, and offered them free reign to search the whole house. They took her up on it. With Dorothea hovering around them, they didn't feel comfortable tearing the whole place up, but even so, Cabrera was able to add a few more concerning threads to his tapestry of guilt: the books that Dorothea had lying around about the properties of drugs, with dog-eared pages relating to many of the medications that she'd used in the past for her drugging and robberies. The house was cluttered with the knickknacks and doilies that would've been expected in the home of the elderly woman that Dorothea had been pretending to be. But, with her new facelift and her false teeth in place, she no longer matched the appearance that she'd been using as a mask all this time.

Among the many prescription medications in her name, hidden away in her room behind her extravagant perfumes and makeup, there was a single bottle labelled for Dorothy Miller. When Cabrera asked her about it, Dorothea explained that Dorothy, her sister-in-law, had come to visit and must've left the bottle behind. It was a logical enough explanation, but it still rang false to Cabrera. After a few hours, they'd been through the whole house with no evidence worse than an unpleasant smell lingering around her bedroom, which she attributed to a dead rat beneath the floorboards and feigned embarrassment about. They had nothing at all to go on beyond that one misplaced drug bottle.

It was enough for Cabrera. He pushed his luck and asked for Dorothea's permission to have a dig around in her garden, concerned that some evidence may have been lost when Dorothea buried trash out there, as she claimed to have. It would've been quite reasonable for her to refuse, and the police would have had no recourse — there was nowhere near the amount of evidence that would've been required to get a warrant for them to dig up the garden, and her well-known pride in that garden would've provided her with the perfect excuse to refuse them. But, there would still be suspicion. If she had refused, every one of the policemen on her doorstep would go away with the seed of doubt about her innocence planted in their minds, and she couldn't abide that. She couldn't live in a world where people thought that she was a killer. It didn't fit with the stories she told about herself, and to herself. She'd lived in her own fantasy for so long that it's hard to say whether she truly believed that when the police went digging in her garden, there would be nothing to find, or if she'd just greatly overestimated her ability to cover her tracks. Either way, she didn't just give the police permission to dig in the fresh, turned soil of her yard, she also gave them her shovel, since they hadn't brought along enough for everybody.

Cabrera started by the new tree and the freshest patch of churned-up earth, hoping for a quick win and an early end to the day. It was slow going. As he went, the first of the buried trash began to surface: scraps of cloth, little bits of plastic wrapper, something that looked a lot like leather but, on closer examination, revealed to have a texture like beef jerky. The deeper the men dug, the more bits and pieces of this buried trash heap were dragged up and out onto the lawn. Eventually, it seems that they hit an impasse. There was some tough tree root down at the bottom of their excavation, and nobody could shift it, no matter how hard they hacked with the blades of their shovels. It fell to the lead detective himself to fling himself in the hole and pull at the thick root with all of his strength. Wiping sweat and flecks of the beef jerky from his face, Cabrera locked his arms around the root and strained with his whole body, back arching with effort, and the buttons of his muddied shirt threatening to shoot off. For one long moment, they waited in silence, the only sound being Cabrera's grunts and puffs. Then, the root gave away, and he fell back into the mud, a human shin bone still grasped between his aching fingers.

He scrambled out of the hole, dropping the remains behind him, his heart hammering in his chest. The sweat of his efforts washed away in a cold sluice of terror. There was a dead body in the ground. He'd been pulling at a leg. He'd torn a leg from a corpse. The other police pressed forward, and a gasp rolled out amongst them. Where the 'root' had disappeared into the earth before, they could now clearly see a foot in a shoe, hauled up out of the earth by Cabrera's efforts. They turned as one to Dorothea and were startled at the rictus of shock on her face, grossly exaggerated by her massive glasses and the hands pressing at her already hollowed cheeks. She looked like a caricature version of somebody who was shocked more than she did a real person.

The Hunt for Dorothea Puente

To an outside observer, it may have seemed bizarre that Cabrera didn't try to arrest Dorothea on the spot, but there were factors to consider. The street where Dorothea lived had been the location of many homesteads in the early days of Sacramento's history, a place where the proud but poor might very well have buried their dead in their own back yards rather than allow them to be consigned to some potter's field. He'd encountered similar inexplicable bodies several times in his career. More pressingly, he was here to look for the body of Alvaro Montoya, a man who'd only been missing for a few weeks at most. There was no way that Bert could've decomposed down to nothing but bones in the time that he'd been gone. This body and the crime that Dorothea was suspected of didn't match. Even before his crew got brought in and excavated the rest of the remains, Cabrera knew that it couldn't be the body that he was looking for.

He sat Dorothea down in her living room and tried to settle her nerves with a coffee, but she had the appearance of somebody in shock. All of the hard-won colour drained from her face, all of the age she'd paid to have sliced away coming back to haunt her once more. She couldn't understand where the body had come from. She couldn't understand what was happening. Her whole world looked like it was falling apart at the seams, as though this whole day had just been one long, bad dream and she would wake tomorrow to her usual life.

Cabrera left Dorothea hunched over herself inside, stationed some officers in the back yard to keep an eye on things and make sure nobody touched their crime scene, then set off to the courthouse. With the body that they'd discovered, he would have no trouble acquiring a warrant to haul up the rest of Dorothea's garden, and even less trouble soliciting cash from the department to hire in a backhoe to do the majority of the heavy lifting.

The next day was a Saturday, but nobody had a single complaint about working through their weekend. A squad of forensic investigators descended on the back garden and started hauling up the remains that the team from Friday had discovered at a rapid pace. To Cabrera's horror, they explained that the flecks of leathery substance that he'd mistaken for jerky was actually mummified human flesh. Because the body had been buried in such an unusual way, it hadn't putrefied and rotted as might have been expected. Instead, the remains had dried out, and fragments of it had been distributed throughout the soil by the repeated disruption by Dorothea, her gardeners and Cabrera's detectives. Worse still, the remains weren't that of Alvaro Montoya as they had initially hoped but from an unknown, older woman. It would only be much later that she was finally formally identified as Leona Carpenter.

As the digging continued, Dorothea watched from the window, saying nothing to anyone. She watched as they pulled up her lawn and made their way across towards the gazebo that she'd recently had erected over the concrete slab that Chief had laid out for her. She could see where they were heading next, and now that the illusion of her innocence was shattered, she could work out exactly whose body they would uncover next. She'd clung to her own stories to make it easier to get through the day — it was much simpler for her to repeat the lie if she believed it, so she'd committed to believing every one of her lies wholeheartedly. Now that was gone, sanity prevailed, and action was required. There were only minutes, at best, before another body was uncovered and any possibility of passing this off as a coincidence would vanish. She had to move, now.

Dressed in her finest red clothes, with her purse stuffed to bursting with almost $4,000 in cash and her very best umbrella dangling on her wrist, Dorothea strolled out into the backyard, weaving through the swarming police and forensics experts to reach Detective Cabrera, where he was overlooking the latest pit that the backhoe had opened up. 'Am I under arrest?'

Cabrera was startled by the old woman's silent approach, but he could tell from the haunted expression on her face that this was all getting to be too much for her, watching her home and the garden that had been her pride and joy being torn apart. Sympathy tempered his answer. 'Of course not, Mrs Puente.'

'So, I am free to go? I can go to the hotel and have a coffee? I need to calm down.'

Cabrera put an arm around her shoulders. 'Don't worry about a thing. I will drive you there myself.'

At the front of the house, a massive crowd had gathered: locals, reporters and all of the usual miscellaneous hangers-on that accompany any sort of excitement in a big city. Questions were flung at Cabrera and Dorothea, but she kept her head down at his request, and he got her to the car and the hotel safely. He told her just to give him a call when she was ready to come home and he'd send someone around for her. Then he left her there.

Dorothea stood still until the detective's car was out of sight, then she called a taxi to take her across town. She stopped at a dive bar that she was known to frequent, to drink a couple of vodka and orange juices to settle her nerves, then she put her plan of action into effect without any more delay. The money in her purse would last her a fair while, and she could afford to throw some of it around if it made her trail a little harder to follow. She booked a plane ticket to Los Angeles, paying with cash, then took the shuttle bus from the airport back into town, switching to a Greyhound bus at the central depot and heading to LA cross-country, instead.

She had years of talking shop with the upper echelons of the police department to fuel her escape plans. She'd heard all about how easy it was for them to identify when a plane ticket hadn't been used, and she manipulated that system to make it seem like there was no way that she could have been heading for Los Angeles. It was the kind of twisted genius that had helped her evade capture throughout all of the preceding years, the perfect grasp of human psychology that let her manipulate everyone around her with ease.

Once she arrived in downtown LA, her old stomping grounds, she set herself up in room 31 of the Royal Viking Motel under the name Dorothea Johansson, then went out on the prowl for a more permanent residence. She'd never had trouble attracting male attention, even in her later years, and, dressed in all her finery, strolling around in a cloud of expensive perfume, she seemed very much like the celebrity that she'd always claimed to be. Heads turned as she walked into the bar, and when she started knocking back screwdrivers as if they were nothing, more than one man began to suspect he might be in for an exciting night. There were a half dozen men who took her fancy, men who were old enough to have retired but young enough that they might believe in her interest. If her thoughts turned to the events back home, then she never let it show.

Just minutes after Dorothea left home, the circus outside the fences had kicked into overdrive. Even more news trucks had arrived, completely blocking F Street. Local residents had started climbing the fences to peer inside the garden. By the time that Cabrera arrived back at the house, he had to go on foot from more than a block away, and even when waving his badge around he had to elbow his way through. He'd no sooner arrived than the frenzy kicked up another notch. Using the backhoe to lever up the concrete, which had been laid down in the back yard, had revealed more graves, and now the bodies were being hauled out. Without the disruption of the shovels, they came out in one piece; each one bound up in their cocoons of cloth and plastic, all decomposing in the same strange way as a result. Any suggestion of an innocent explanation had vanished the moment that another body appeared, and over the following four hours, the crew diligently uncovered and documented the crop of corpses planted across Dorothea's gardens. Seven bodies were taken away to the morgue for examination, and the forensic teams on site were flung into the house in search of an explanation. To the horror of the police, the watch on the wrist of one of the fresher bodies was still ticking. If they'd responded faster to concerns about Bert's disappearance, Dorothea might have been stopped before that last woman was killed.

Inside the house, everything looked as perfect and pristine as always. Every detail had to be documented, every hint at the truth filed away to ensure a conviction. Raking through all of the papers in the house gradually revealed the list of non-residents that Dorothea was still banking cheques for, a list considerably longer than the number of bodies that had been found out in the garden. This was their shortlist for identifying bodies and the perfect motive for Dorothea to have killed her residents. Greed.

Still, they pressed on through the rest of the house, documenting every scratch on the woodwork or stain on the carpet, sending so many samples out for testing to the local forensic labs for weeks to follow. The books on drugs and their uses, along with Dorothea's massive stockpile of prescription medication, provided them with an obvious method of murder, but still, things weren't adding up. Where was she killing her victims? The reports from long-time residents of the boarding house had indicated that she often took people up to her rooms, who'd then vanish overnight. So, it was there that the team focused their efforts, but if the rest of the house looked pristine, Dorothea's rooms looked downright polished, a luxury apartment stowed away on top of the rather drab fixtures of the lower levels, with the bouquet of her many perfumes still hanging thick in the air. More documents and more drugs were found around the rooms, squirrelled away in unexpected places, but still no clear sign of any forensic evidence that might tie Dorothea directly to the murders. It was only when they peeled back the veneer of civilisation that they could discover the truth. Dorothea's bed was still in perfect condition thanks to the careful replacement of sheets and blankets, and her carpets were so pristine they looked as though they hadn't even been tread on before the forensics team arrived. It was like a showroom, and that in itself was suspicious. The team lifted the carpet in Dorothea's bedroom, and suddenly, the source of the foul smell became clear. Even after all of these years, some small part of Dorothea remained the same feral child who'd never learned to clean up properly. She had lain fresh carpet over the stains on the wooden boards below, never even considering that it might be wise to wash them. From her bed to the hallway, there was a long, dark smear of bodily fluids, a trail of decay leading straight down and towards the garden. It couldn't have been any more obvious what had happened — if Dorothea had been there to talk the investigators through it.

In the chaos of the discovery of the bodies and all of the rushing about, Dorothea's disappearance wasn't noted until four hours after she'd already slunk off. With horror, Cabrera dispatched a squad car to pick her up or scour the streets for her if she'd left the hotel, but there was no sign of the old woman anywhere. It was like she'd vanished into thin air, and he had helped her. With no small amount of shame following him, he went out to address the media and to kick off one of the strangest manhunts in American history.

The press and the public couldn't believe that Dorothea Puente, the adorable little old lady who cared for stray cats, helped the homeless and gave out her homemade tamales, could possibly be a murderer. Even when the FBI was drafted in for assistance, there was an air of amusement permeating their efforts. Still, Cabrera drove it ever onwards, painfully aware that it was only a matter of time before Dorothea killed again. The sheer volume of bodies in the house showed that she had no intention of stopping, and her sudden loss of income would drive her to it if the motive was entirely financial. They had to catch her before it was too late.

The unique manner in which Dorothea had prepared the bodies prior to burial made it all too easy to connect the John Doe murder from several months before to her, and only a little reading through her correspondence clued the police in to the fact that she was maintaining the façade that Everson Gillmouth was still alive to his family. With some idea of who their mystery body was, it took only a swift exhumation and an examination of some x-rays to confirm their suspicions. The other bodies were not so quick to be identified. It took seven days before names could be attached to every one of them, days during which the whole country was combed for the people on Dorothea's list, when families had to be contacted and warned that their loved one might be among the list of victims and that Dorothea Puente was still at large. For the families of her confirmed victims, this news was something like vindication. William Clausen, Ruth Monroe's son, had long suspected that Dorothea was behind his mother's death, and now that the bodies discovered in her back garden had been proven to contain lethal quantities of the same drug that had killed Ruth, he was apoplectic with rage. Everson's children were similarly furious, although they turned that rage inwards, blaming themselves instead of lashing out and making public statements.

The hunt ranged from the northern states, which Dorothea had once called home, all the way down to Mexico, where it was assumed she would have fled as she had the last time the police were closing in on her. Her face was on the news hourly and in newspapers around the world. Yet, still in downtown LA, she managed to pass by unnoticed in the dimly lit bars that she frequented. Three days on the lam was more than enough for Dorothea — she wanted to get back to her home comforts, which meant first acquiring a home. Charles Willgues was her target of choice, as she'd flirted her way through a great many of the local men with little luck. She introduced herself to him as Donna Johansson, and before long, the conversation turned to her latest story.

Her bag had been lost or stolen on arrival in Los Angeles, and she was completely without clothing to wear. Even the heels that she was wearing were getting run down from all the walking she had to do. Taking pity on her, Charles led her over the street to a cobbler, whom he paid to do some repair work on her shoes. Donna was most impressed with his generosity, asking how he came by money to spare. He explained that he received disability benefits. At once, her face lit up, and she started telling him about all the supplemental benefits he was probably entitled to but didn't know about. He was amazed by the breadth of her knowledge, if a little perplexed as to how a woman who was so obviously well-off knew so much about the United States benefits system. She was soon pressing him for details about his living situation, trying to finagle herself an invitation back to his place. At first, he thought that she was just incredibly forward, but gradually, he realised that she seemed considerably more interested in his home than she was in him. A few little alarm bells were ringing in his mind as he walked her back to the Royal Viking, but they parted on good terms, with Charles offering to take her about town the next day to buy some replacement clothes.

It was only when he got home that his suspicions began to fester. There was no way that his Donna was the Dorothea woman who was on the news all the time. Even if she was weirdly fascinated with his benefits and a bit pushy with her demands that they start living together, that didn't mean she was a murderess on the run. He didn't have the confidence to call the police about the situation, but the local press was another matter entirely. He was fairly sure he'd seen Donna on the news that morning, but he couldn't be certain, so he called them up and ended up speaking to CBS Editor, Gene Silver. Silver asked him to watch the next news bulletin to check the picture but then got a call back when CBS failed to show the picture during that broadcast. Sensing that a story was afoot, Silver drove around to visit Charles himself, bringing a photo of Dorothea along for positive identification. It only took Charles one look to be certain. Dorothea Puente was Donna.

The next morning, Dorothea was awakened by a hammering on her motel door. When she opened it, she was momentarily dazzled by the flashing of camera bulbs. The press had found her, and there was no way that they were going to take a step back now that she was being arrested. The officer on the scene asked 'Donna' for some identification and, cornered with no time to think, she handed over her own. Dorothea Puente was arrested and put onto a flight back home the same day, chartered by The Sacramento Bee newspaper. The whole flight home, she was surrounded by the press, hounded with questions. For the first time, she had no story to spin and no desire for the attention. All that they got from her throughout the whole journey was the half-hearted beginning of a denial, 'I cashed the cheques, yes. But, I never killed anyone', and the somewhat more sinister confession: 'I used to be a good person, once'.

The Trials of Dorothea Puente

The Sacramento police took charge of Dorothea on the runway, leading her directly to Sacramento County Jail, where she was booked in promptly. It was only here that her property was searched and documented, and the $3,000 that she had leftover from her escape attempt was discovered in her bulging purse. That very same morning, she was brought before the court to meet her appointed lawyers, Peter Vlautin and Kevin Clymo — the men who'd been given the onerous task of keeping Dorothea Puente, known around the world as a mass murderer, out of jail. There was a session of court lasting only seven minutes, during which Dorothea was arraigned without bail for one count of murder.

Bert Montoya, the man whom she thought nobody cared about, had brought the full weight of justice down on her.

In jail, Dorothea enjoyed none of the companionship that she was accustomed to in prison. The whole world knew about her crimes, and people couldn't meet her eye. She had nobody to tell her stories to, except for her lawyers, and lying to them just got her rolled eyes and sighs. The police were taking months to piece together the case that the prosecution were going to use to pin every death on Dorothea, but they were being exceptionally thorough about it. Every lie that she told would be another nail in her coffin as far as the defence were concerned. They had no way of knowing just how much of Dorothea's history had already been uncovered, so every time she spun one of her tall tales and it was disproved, it ruined her credibility. Still, even in these private and confidential meetings with her lawyers, Dorothea couldn't bring herself to acknowledge the truth. She insisted on her innocence, insisted that her patchwork quilt of personal history was the absolute truth, and doubled down on any lie that she was caught in. Eventually, Vlautin and Clymo realised that the only way they were going to keep their client out of prison was to keep her off the stand. The whole trial was going to have to proceed without Dorothea speaking up in her own defence.

The sweet old lady act that Dorothea had been using for years was going to be her lawyers' first line of emotional attack on the jury, and with that angle destroyed, they went for the next best thing — character witnesses, and plenty of them. They reached out to everyone in the communities that Dorothea had helped, all of the homeless people who were given a secured home, all of the neighbours who'd eaten her tamales or watched her caring for stray cats and stray men alike, the single mothers who'd found a way to escape their abusive husbands. Every life that Dorothea had touched was rolled out as a shield in front of her, and the grandest lie of all was built out of it. The ways that Dorothea had spent her ill-gotten gains on charitable work were well documented, so Vlautin and Clymo leaned into that as an explanation. Dorothea gave care to people who were close to death every day, and when they did finally expire, she used the money that was due to them to help others. Her statement on the plane became their entire defence. 'I cashed the cheques, but I didn't kill them'.

Meanwhile, the prosecution had decided to drop the fraud charges related to Dorothea's complex benefits scams for fear that the jury would get too confused if they had to explain all the ins and outs of the systems that were being exploited. The murders were the charges on which Dorothea was indicted, and they were what the prosecution planned to nail her on. It was all or nothing.

On 25th April 1990, pre-trial hearings began. The court was packed to bursting with the media and members of the public, a massive audience waiting to see if justice would be done. The prosecution launched into their narrative, describing Dorothea as a cold-blooded, calculating murderer, who'd established her boarding house business to prey on the weak and helpless of society for her own monetary gain. The defence didn't engage with that story, instead putting forward a motion to move the trial. The trial had become a media event, and the coverage that Dorothea had received so far was guaranteed to have prejudiced any jury in the area against her. Judge Gail Ohanesian sat through two days of arguments from both sides before finally ruling that a change of venue was acceptable, but that there would be no mistrial on the basis of media coverage. Despite the massive public interest, she'd seen no evidence that the trial would violate Dorothea's constitutional rights.

Arguments and evidence were presented in the weeks and months that followed, and everything that would later be relied on in the jury trial was presented to the judge, including the copious statements from the psychologists, whom her lawyers had brought in to interview Dorothea in the vague hope of an insanity defence. Those psychologists argued that Dorothea's childhood and unstable life up until recently could've contributed to her stress levels when residents died in her care. They believed that this might have affected her decision making and that the fear of her stable life being torn apart led to her hiding the bodies rather than reporting their deaths. Because of the terms of her parole, it was possible that she'd never reported the deaths because it might have led to her being jailed. In the end, nine counts of murder were filed against her, and the jury trial was set to take place in Monterey.

It took many months to find an unbiased jury, and even longer for the many different motions put forward by the defence to be picked apart. They were playing for time. The longer that the jury had to wait, the more likely they would forget details of the media coverage. They did that job well. It was 9th February 1993, before the trial finally began.

Both sides presented their same cases as previous, the prosecution arguing that Dorothea was a monster, the defence that she was a saint. 153 different witnesses were called to give evidence. 3,500 pages of reports were offered up. A scale model of the boarding house on F Street was wheeled out into the courtroom. Delay after delay after delay was introduced, making this trial into the longest in California history. On 15th July, the jury withdrew to consider the evidence and present their verdict, well aware that the prosecution were seeking the death penalty for the little old lady who was perched behind the bench beside them.

Nobody knows exactly what happened in the room where the jurors were gathered, whether there were arguments, confusion, persuasion or anything else — those rooms are sealed — but, after days of deliberation, a note was passed back to the judge on 2nd August. 'We, the jury, are deadlocked on all nine counts — we would like further instructions'.

The defence immediately demanded that this be ruled a mistrial, but Judge Michael J Virga fended them off, instead telling his jury to go back and try again, after providing them with very clear instructions on how to achieve a decision. It took until 26th August before they finally came back with a decision, and even then, it was incomplete. They were still deadlocked on most of the counts, with only three that they were willing to convict Dorothea on: the murders of Dorothy Miller and Ben Fink in the first degree, and of Leona Carpenter in the second degree.

Dorothea took the news with the same stone-faced acceptance with which she had viewed pictures of her victims, both alive and decomposed, throughout the trial. It was only when the judge handed down her sentence of life without parole that she finally spoke. 'I didn't kill anyone'.

William Clausen, the son of Ruth Monroe, was satisfied when he heard that justice was finally being done, even if his mother's death was never officially treated as a murder. When reporters asked him if he was upset that Dorothea had not received the death penalty, he explained that he was not. There were only two ways that Dorothea's life could end now. She would either die in prison or somehow find a way to trick the system and escape. Then, he would be waiting for her.

Dorothea was sent to the women's prison in Chowchilla, where she lived out the rest of her days in exactly the kind of quiet celebrity that she'd always desired. She denied all of her crimes but relished the attention and respect that she received for having committed them. Everyone in Chowchilla knew who she was and would say hello to her politely.

She was 64 years old by the time that she was locked up for the last time, and as the years rolled on, she made her way through all of the different jobs in the prison before age and infirmity finally took that business from her. Towards the end, she would still rise with the dawn to clean her entire shared cell and make use of the $10 monthly donation that she received from an unnamed charity to produce home-made snacks for her cellmates and the guards. When 'Miss Dorothea' was cooking, the whole block livened up, hoping for a taste.

Towards the end of her life, she filled more and more of her time with fiction, reading crime thrillers and watching CSI, Criminal Minds and Cold Case on television, obsessing over fictional murders while still maintaining that she'd committed none herself.

Whenever services were held in the prison chapel, she would attend, but she avoided formally joining any inmate worship groups for fear of being asked to confess her sins. Religion had been a defining cornerstone of Dorothea's life as a child, with the church providing her with the care and stability that her parents refused to, so it is of no surprise that, in her final days, she turned to God once more. But for forgiveness to be received, guilt first has to be admitted, and Dorothea couldn't tell the truth of what she'd done, even until the very end. Her stories, her precious lies that she'd worn with such pride and delight, were still wrapped around her like gilded chains to the very last moment of her life. She would never admit to any of her crimes. She wouldn't even admit to having lived her actual life. She still claimed to be receiving mail from celebrities and ex-husbands who'd long moved on with their lives and forgotten her name.

On 27th March 2011, at the grand old age of 82, Dorothea died of natural causes in her cell in Chowchilla. The same natural causes that she claimed had taken all of her victims, even up until her final moments on this planet.

About the Author

Ryan Green is a true crime author in his late thirties. He lives in Herefordshire, England with his wife, three children, and two dogs. Outside of writing and spending time with his family, Ryan enjoys walking, reading and windsurfing.

Ryan is fascinated with History, Psychology and True Crime. In 2015, he finally started researching and writing his own work and at the end of the year, he released his first book on Britain's most notorious serial killer, Harold Shipman.

He has since written several books on lesser-known subjects, and taken the unique approach of writing from the killer's perspective. He narrates some of the most chilling scenes you'll encounter in the True Crime genre.

You can sign up to Ryan's newsletter to receive a free book, updates, and the latest releases at:

WWW.RYANGREENBOOKS.COM

More Books by Ryan Green

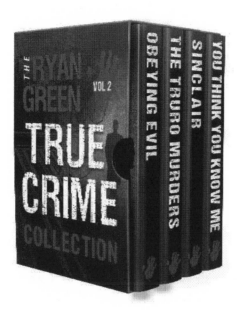

4 books for the price of 2 (save 50%)

Four chilling true crime stories in one collection, from the bestselling author Ryan Green.

Volume 2 contains some of Green's most fascinating accounts of violence, abuse, deception and murder. Within this collection, you'll receive:

- Obeying Evil
- The Truro Murders
- Sinclair
- You Think You Know Me

More Books by Ryan Green

In 1902, at the age of 11, Carl Panzram broke into a neighbour's home and stole some apples, a pie, and a revolver. As a frequent troublemaker, the court decided to make an example of him and placed him into the care of the Minnesota State Reform School. During his two-year detention, Carl was repeatedly beaten, tortured, humiliated and raped by the school staff.

At 15-years old, Carl enlisted in the army by lying about his age but his career was short-lived. He was dishonourably discharged for stealing army supplies and was sent to military prison. The brutal prison system sculpted Carl into the man that he would remain for the rest of his life. He hated the whole of mankind and wanted revenge.

When Carl left prison in 1910, he set out to rob, burn, rape and kill as many people as he could, for as long as he could. His campaign of terror could finally begin and nothing could stand in his way.

More Books by Ryan Green

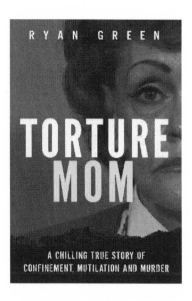

In July 1965, teenagers Sylvia and Jenny Likens were left in the temporary care of Gertrude Baniszewski, a middle-aged single mother and her seven children.

The Baniszewski household was overrun with children. There were few rules and ample freedom. Sadly, the environment created a dangerous hierarchy of social Darwinism where the strong preyed on the weak.

What transpired in the following three months was both riveting and chilling. The case shocked the entire nation and would later be described as "The single worst crime perpetuated against an individual in Indiana's history".

Free True Crime Audiobook

Listen to four chilling True Crime stories in one collection. Follow the link below to download a FREE copy of *The Ryan Green True Crime Collection: Vol. 3.*

WWW.RYANGREENBOOKS.COM/FREE-AUDIOBOOK

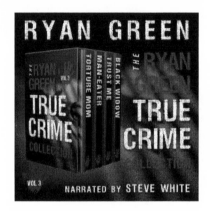

"Ryan Green has produced another excellent book and belongs at the top with true crime writers such as M. William Phelps, Gregg Olsen and Ann Rule" –**B.S. Reid**

"Wow! Chilling, shocking and totally riveting! I'm not going to sleep well after listening to this but the narration was fantastic. Crazy story but highly recommend for any true crime lover!" –**Mandy**

"Torture Mom by Ryan Green left me pretty speechless. The fact that it's a true story is just...wow" –**JStep**

"Graphic, upsetting, but superbly read and written" –**Ray C**

WWW.RYANGREENBOOKS.COM/FREE-AUDIOBOOK